The
Nightingale
of
Mosul

The Nightingale of Mosul

A Nurse's Journey of Service, Struggle, and War

SUSAN LUZ

WITH

MARCUS BROTHERTON

PUBLISHING

New York

© 2010 by Susan Luz

Published by Kaplan Publishing, a division of Kaplan, Inc.
1 Liberty Plaza, 24th Floor
New York, NY 10006

Printed in the United States of America.

10 9 8 7 6 5 4 3 2

Library of Congress Cataloging-in-Publication Data has been applied for.

ISBN: 978-1-60714-631-5

Kaplan Publishing books are available at special quantity discounts to use for sales promotions, employee premiums, or educational purposes. For more information or to order books, please call the Simon & Schuster special sales department at 866-506-1949.

Dear Anne,

In war, I fought the battles every day
and _hoped_ I'd win.

My nephews—Geoffrey, Matthew, and Ryan—
fight their battles against Cystic Fibrosis every day,
but I _know_ they will win!

_Oh, what a life I've had!
I hope you enjoy my book.
All my best to you,
Susan
(Colonel Susan Luz Ret)_

CONTENTS

PROLOGUE

My hands shook slightly with adrenaline when the letter arrived from the Department of the Army, on March 30, 2006. I unfolded it, already anticipating what it would say.

After reading it carefully, I folded it back up, sat at the kitchen counter, and looked out the window for a long time, squinting into the late-afternoon Rhode Island fog. The letter announced that my Army Reserve unit had been officially activated for mobilization in support of Operation Iraqi Freedom, and I would soon be deployed to Iraq for up to 545 days.

This was the letter I had been waiting for my whole life. I welcomed it, yet I dreaded it. I welcomed it because I have built my life around serving others. I dreaded it because it meant a year and a half in a combat zone, a year and a half away from home, husband, family, all that I loved. If I was lucky, that's all the time it would be, and I would come home safe when our tour was up. If I was unlucky, I would come home sooner, ironically, wounded by some sniper's rifle. If I was unluckier still, well, there was always the option I wouldn't come home at all.

I took a deep breath and put the letter in a safe place that I'd remember. I needed to give it to my employer the next day, the pragmatic next step in the process. When you've been a nurse for as long as I have, you prepare yourself for these things. You learn and live by the maxim that a life of serving others leads to a sense of purpose. Any type of service, if it's worth doing, usually involves some kind of difficulty; some kind of pain emerges in the process. There lay my inner conflict. I wanted to help. I truly did. But I had no idea what kind of pain lay ahead. I feared the worst.

I looked around my kitchen for something to do, something to keep my hands busy while I thought this out. In times of stress my first inclination is to make something gooey and chocolaty and delicious and horrible—maybe chocolate fudge brownies with extra icing. I'd devour the pan and then bake another, and all would be right with the world. But that would never do. For the sake of the bathroom scale, I decided to avoid this type of stress reliever.

Grabbing a scrub brush and spray bottle, I went to work on my stove. It was past due for a solid scouring. Though I wanted to help in Iraq, nobody actually wants to go to *war*. Even as necessary as some wars are, I thought as I polished, I certainly didn't want to go.

Take someone you care deeply about and shoot his body full of holes. Blow him up when his vehicle drives over an improvised explosive device. Burn his ear so it sticks to the side of his head. Use a Shop-Vac to suck his blood off an emergency room floor. Those are the kinds of things I knew I would see in Iraq in the days ahead. I set down the scrub brush. In my fervor I was scrubbing the enamel off my stove.

I sat down on a kitchen chair, brushing a wisp of graying blond hair from my face. For one brief moment, I toyed with the idea of getting excused from active duty. At 56, I made for a pretty old soldier. I definitely could have played my age card or drummed up some other excuse if I put my mind to it. Some reservists do. When the crunch time comes, there are always a few who want to drop out. They initially joined the reserves for the extra cash, for the adventure of providing quick response to natural disasters, or for help with university expenses. But the main point of being a reservist is to be ready to go to war if the need arises.

I shook the idea of quitting out of my mind. Since its formation in 1908, the U.S. Army Reserve has served with honor in every one of the nation's major military engagements for the past century: World War I, World War II, the Korean War, the Vietnam War, the cold war, the 1989 invasion of Panama, the 1990–91 Persian Gulf War, the civil war in Somalia, the 1992–95 war in Bosnia and Herzegovina, the 1998–99 conflict in Kosovo, the 2004 Haitian rebellion, the war in Afghanistan begun in 2001, and the Iraq War begun in 2003. We never know where the next unrest in the world might occur, but most reservists I know are confident we'll be able to help no matter what the task. That was the organization I was part of. I wouldn't let my country down.

Yet my hands were still shaking slightly—and maybe it wasn't from excitement. Maybe it was plain, cold terror fighting to overrule my decision to join my unit in its deployment to Iraq. No matter how firm my resolve, I knew there was dangerous country ahead.

PART ONE

Gearing Up

CHAPTER I

Dangerous Country Ahead

MY HUSBAND, GEORGE, pushed the peas around on his plate at dinner. He's usually in a great mood, ever cheerful, but I knew he was chewing on the realities of what the letter meant for us.

"You know I'll support whatever you do," he said at last.

I reached over the table and laid my hand on top of his. I knew. The thought that I would see George again was a huge part of what would keep me going while I was away. Sure, I wanted to go to Iraq and serve. I was motivated by the notion of doing my duty, perhaps even by the promise of adventure that lay ahead. But more than anything else, I envisioned coming home at the end of the tour and holding George in a close embrace. I wanted to come home again safely and live out the rest of my days with the man I loved. It was a simple goal, perhaps, yet one I would hold to tightly in the days and months to come.

Later that evening, I got in my car and drove out on the wet freeways from our house in North Scituate, Rhode Island, to the hospital in Boston where my nephew Geoffrey lay. The windshield wipers beat a hypnotic rhythm against the night rain of early spring.

Geoffrey is like a son to George and me. I left my umbrella in the car, took the elevator to the hospital's fourth floor, and paused for a moment, dripping against the closed door of Geoffrey's room. It wouldn't have surprised me if the news behind the door was bleak. I should have called first, but I needed to be there in person.

Patients with the type of lung transplant that my nephew had just received are given less than a 10 percent chance of survival. This was actually his second transplant, and I knew tonight might be the last time I saw Geoffrey alive. I expected the worst, but I wasn't ready to give up on him.

I drew on my solid belief in hard work and God, the two key pillars of my life. I believe that God helps those who help themselves and that when we ask him to help us, he's seldom in the habit of disappointing. I tossed a Hail Mary down the field. "Our God, who art in heaven," I prayed, still leaning against the door, "I know you're not much into bargains, but here's my deal: Geoffrey has been so brave for so long. If you let Geoffrey survive this thing, then I'll go to Iraq and do the best job I can. I'll go for his sake, as well as yours."

I opened the door. Geoffrey's six-foot frame lay in bed motionless, and his blondish-brown hair draped over his handsome face, bloated from prednisone. When he was young, Geoffrey, now 23, had been diagnosed with cystic fibrosis, a life-shortening disease that attacks the mucus glands of the lungs. He had never considered himself handicapped, however; he was always smiling and threw himself headlong into whatever challenge lay before him. He had graduated from Boston College and conducted himself in every interaction like the captain of a basketball team.

It seemed longer than a week ago that we had received a call that a new pair of lungs was ready. The bittersweet news came at 3:00 A.M. Recipients are never told any specifics about organ donors, but the lungs were already racing across the country in flight. Geoffrey was rushed to Boston for the transplant. My nephew had looked so frail then. For weeks he had been wheezing, his weight down. Each breath came with a struggle.

Now after the transplant, I leaned over Geoffrey's recovery bed and kissed his cheek lightly. As I sat down next to her, Geoffrey's mother—my sister, Ellen-Ann—took my hand, still wet from the rain. Ellen-Ann nodded, a slight smile tugging at the corners of her mouth. She wore a strange look of triumph, but she wasn't saying anything just yet. Still, I had a hunch.

"Really?" I asked.

"His breathing's improving," Ellen-Ann nodded. "His color's getting better every hour. Doctors are starting to say he might just pull through."

I hugged my sister. She hugged me back. That's all the good news we would whisper to each other just then. God was answering yes to my prayer, at least for today. Geoffrey was going to make it.

This was the confirmation I was looking for. Geoffrey's survival would become my inspiration for going to Iraq. I figured if Geoffrey could fight his good fight as he had been doing, then my calling was similarly to press forward. If my presence in Iraq could in any way help just one mother keep her son alive, then I could certainly find the courage to fulfill my duty as an Army Reserve nurse. I resolved that no matter how dangerous it was, I was going to war. I would push through the danger, do whatever I needed to do to help in Iraq, and then, God willing, come home again to Rhode Island and hug George.

I BELIEVE THAT WHENEVER you vow to do something that calls for guts, your resolve is immediately tested. It's like God wants to check your mettle. He'll help you, sure, through the many prayers you'll whisper to him over the next chunk of time, but he also wants to put his money on a winning horse. If you say you're going to do something extraordinary, God wants you to mean what you say.

It wasn't long before my resolve was tested. That very weekend, just three days after receiving the orders to mobilize, I completed a routine weekend drill with my unit at Hanscom Air Force Base in Massachusetts. It was part of the gear-up for our June 8 deployment. Reservists aren't the same as full-time soldiers. We're regular folks who hold regular jobs outside of our reservist duties. A reservist's responsibility to the military comprises one weekend per month and two additional weeks per year. The rest of the time we do our own thing. So whenever a reserve unit is called up to go into a combat zone, it takes a lot of extra training to get us there.

This particular training weekend went smoothly. My unit— about 450 soldiers—packed up all the medical equipment we'd need, sat in a lot of briefings, and did the usual training runs and last-minute physical testing. There was excitement within the ranks, but there was also an unmistakable get-ready-for-the-worst-case-scenario feeling. We were told to make detailed plans for our spouses showing where everything important was kept in our houses. Attorneys briefed us on getting our wills and life insurance in order.

After the weekend, George picked me up to drive me home. As we crossed the state line back into Rhode Island, signs of spring were everywhere. Blue violets and pink lady's slippers were just beginning to blossom. Warm winds were breezing over from Newport on the coast. We stopped at the cleaner's so I could pick up some dry cleaning. I was still thinking of the good news of Geoffrey's recovery from the transplant. But when I returned to the car with my dry cleaning in hand, George was on his cell phone talking to his sister, Lana. He had a faraway look in his eyes.

"It's Brian," George said softly as he closed the phone. Brian St. Germain, 22, was George's cousin's son, a marine on his second tour of duty in Iraq.

"George, what's wrong?" I asked. "Is everything okay?"

George turned his face to the breeze. He shook his head and didn't say anything. I could see his back shivering. How strange that half a world away such chaos could exist. Our nephew, Geoffrey, would survive to live another day, but Brian, this other boy we loved so much, wouldn't. The bad news seemed implausible on a bright spring day such as this.

Through tears, George filled me in: Brian's young life had been taken in a flash flood. *How tragically ironic,* I thought. *Iraq is a country of 168,000 square miles, with about 167,000 of those square miles being waterless desert—how could Brian have drowned?* Brian and his buddies were on patrol near the Al Asad Airbase, about 100 miles west of Baghdad, when sudden rains turned the roadway into a watercourse. They were driving a seven-ton truck—a huge, armor-plated, six-wheel-drive vehicle—but even with all that weight and power, they were swept away in an instant and lost in the Euphrates River. Drowned in a desert. *Unbelievable.*

A week after the accident, Brian's funeral was held in West Warwick, Rhode Island, the same small town, the same funeral home where services had once been held for George's father, a World War II veteran. Everybody knows everybody else in West Warwick. A line of friends and neighbors stretched down the block. Many of Brian's friends from the U.S. Marine Corps had flown in from Camp Pendleton, in California, where Brian had last been stationed stateside. The police were out in full force in case there were protesters, but there were none. Not today. A line of motorcyclists from the American Freedom Riders were on hand to show their support.

Near the coffin were pictures of Brian at boot camp. Pictures of him in high school. Pictures of him with our family. Brian had just bought a big white Dodge Ram truck that he kept at Pendleton. He loved that truck as much as he loved being a marine. Being in the marines was always his dream—he had enlisted as soon as he graduated from high school.

I took my place in line to pay my last respects. Brian's body had been found in the water right away, and there it was in the open casket, his face looking very peaceful, handsome, in spite of the setting. Rows of medals were pinned to his chest.

I lingered at the casket. I had already heard whispers behind my back. Many well-wishers knew that my reserve unit had been called to Iraq and had already hugged me good-bye as if I weren't coming back. It was as if people sensed anew the danger of war. For everyone in our extended family, Brian's death was a tragic reminder that there are a lot of ways to get injured or killed in a war zone.

As I walked away from the casket, Brian's mother found me and took my hand. I felt something pressed into it, a small gift from a fellow Catholic.

"Keep this on you," she said. What she had placed in my hand was a crocheted angel, an icon of safety to keep with me while in Iraq.

"Thank you," I said and tried to smile. "I'll think of Brian always."

We hugged, Brian's mother and I. And then there were tears from us both.

AS A COLONEL, the highest-ranking female in my unit, the 399th Combat Support Hospital, I would not carry a rifle even in Iraq, like the rest of my unit would, and I would not be in charge of a battalion or a regiment, like a colonel would typically be. I would be there to draw on my work as a public health nurse. When I'm not with the Army Reserve, I work with troubled adolescents at a psychiatric facility.

My unit's job in Iraq was to be the frontline station for troops in the field. When soldiers (and sometimes, unfortunately, civilians) are hit, field medics patch them up as well as possible, then rush the wounded to us via helicopter and Humvee. We are the hospital nearest the battle, a modern-day Mobile Army Surgical Hospital (M*A*S*H) unit. We are the Sherman T. Potters, Margaret Houlihans, and Hawkeye Pierces of the Iraq War.

My specific job within the 399th was to make sure everyone stayed healthy. It was as simple and as complex as that. Taking care of the physical side of things is sometimes the easiest. I was expected to spend a lot of my time in Iraq holding seminars. Soldiers—or anyone else away from home for a time, for that matter—can be notorious for not taking care of themselves, so my job was to make sure they were educated in all sorts of good, healthy-living practices. If they had high blood pressure, I wanted them to knock off the salt. If they smoked, I wanted them to quit. If they were fooling around, I wanted them to protect themselves against sexually transmitted diseases.

But humans are more than physical beings, and as health care professionals, our real task is to care for the whole person. When it comes to mental health, stress is a huge part of a soldier's life as well. Take normal people and put them in abnormal situations, and all sorts of hazardous things can result. I hold an additional certification in combat stress management, so part of my job in Iraq was to help educate soldiers through the stresses of war. If people could, to some degree, process the craziness of what they were going through, it would lift their spirits, help them perform at an optimum level, and be in a better position to sort things out when they got home.

As reservists, we had already been through boot camp as well as monthly and annual training exercises for some time, but our training needed to be intensified to prime us for overseas duty. On June 8, 2006, my unit was activated and went to Hanscom for several days of briefings. Each night I was able to go home, which was an unusual and welcome surprise. Toward the end of the briefing period, a ceremony was held at the Boston Convention Center so that we could officially say good-bye to family and friends. The night after the ceremony, we were to be locked down in a hotel near the base, then flown to Fort McCoy, Wisconsin, the next morning, for three and a half months of extra training. There, the unit would be sharpened into a finely tuned instrument before we headed to Iraq. It's no simple task for the army to prepare 450 reservists to be immersed for a year in a combat zone.

A few thousand friends and family members filed into the convention center for the ceremony. From across the crowd, I spotted George. It had only been hours since we had last seen each other, but already my heart skipped a beat at the thought of being away from him for the next long while.

"I brought you some flowers," George said, dropping his r's, New England accent–style.

He handed me a dozen yellow roses and a small American flag. We kissed hello. George comes from a large Portuguese American family. His father, the late George Luz Sr., fought in World War II with Easy (E) Company, 506th Parachute Infantry Regiment, 101st Airborne Division, the company featured in Stephen Ambrose's 1992 book, *Band of Brothers*, which was made into an HBO miniseries produced by Tom Hanks and Steven Spielberg in 2001. My husband and I stay close to several of the

E Company veterans and frequently attend reunions and special events that honor the men. In about a year, George was set to help lead a tour of European battle sites with E Company veterans Bill Guarnere, Babe Heffron, Frank Perconte, Buck Compton, Rod Bain, and Don Malarkey. As part of the tour, the men were scheduled to stop off at various military bases and hospitals in Germany to encourage the soldiers of Operation Iraqi Freedom. I knew it would be great to meet with those legendary men who had given our country so much, as well as the current soldiers who were following in their footsteps. I wished I could go.

More family and friends began to show up for the ceremony. Acting on the advice of the family readiness officer, someone who knew what she was doing, George began to reserve some seats for our group by putting pieces of paper on chairs. The seats saved, George gathered us together for a picture.

"Smile," he said as we put our arms around one another and hollered, "Chee-ee-eese."

Suddenly, I felt a tap on my shoulder. It was a lieutenant colonel. His face was flushed. "Hey, your husband can't do that," he said.

"What?" I said. "Take a picture?"

"No." The lieutenant colonel's eyebrows lowered as if we had committed the unpardonable sin. "Save seats. Against regulation." His voice stayed flat.

"Hey," I called with a smile, "we're trying to take a family picture over here." A lot of emotion floats around in a send-off ceremony—this is the last time you see any family for quite a while. Plus, there were lots of unsaved seats left in the room.

"You need to move these pieces of paper from the seats—now!" he said.

I felt my cheeks reddening. There's always one of these ferret-faced Frank Burns types in every crowd. I felt my Irish blood rising. Before I could open my mouth, the lieutenant colonel pointed to a small stuffed animal hanging out of my backpack and waved his finger in the air. The bear is named Shaggy and goes everywhere I go. George keeps a stuffed bear named Rosie, and whenever George and I are together, Shaggy and Rosie always sit on the same dresser. Whenever George and I are apart, Shaggy and Rosie remind us to count the days until we're together again.

"And that," the lieutenant colonel uttered and pointed again at Shaggy, "is against *regulation*." He accentuated the word like it was gospel truth. "You can't have that hanging out of your backpack."

I couldn't believe this guy. Here we were trying to win a war for freedom, and he wanted to question a stuffed animal. I shifted tactics and moved my shoulder so the lieutenant colonel could see my Eagle, the patch that signifies rank. A lieutenant colonel is one down in rank from a full-bird colonel.

"I don't think there'll be a problem here," I said. I smiled as sweetly as possible.

The lieutenant colonel folded his arms across his chest and shook his head. His final answer.

My smile faded into steel. Nobody pushes me around.

"You want me to pull rank?" I glowered up at him. "If you want me to act army, I'll act army. You know as well as I do that if a lieutenant colonel talks to a colonel like that, he's up for a court-martial. Your decision—what's it going to be?"

The lieutenant colonel huffed, pivoted on his foot, and marched off. In my book, that type of petty policy pushing has no place in a winning army. It felt good to win this small war before I got into the real thing.

Our unit's commander, Colonel Bryan Kelly, spoke at the ceremony, as did Charlie Fogarty, the lieutenant governor of

Rhode Island. A minister pronounced a blessing. The ceremony wasn't long. Many of us had tears in our eyes as they played Lee Greenwood's song "God Bless the USA." I think the seriousness of what we were about to do hit us all in waves. For me, I suddenly didn't want to be alone. I wanted as many friends around me as possible. The *Band of Brothers* idea about needing comrades in arms is completely true. If you're faced with the possibility of shedding your own blood, you want your brothers—or sisters—with you in the fight.

The next morning, after our night in lockdown, we grabbed our gear and lined up to file onto the chartered flight to Fort McCoy. Gear stowed, I still carried the yellow roses that George had given me. Senior officers are always placed in first class. I took my seat next to the window. The spacious seat next to me was empty. This wasn't going to be much fun, flying alone. My good buddy Captain Michele Diamond, a real character, was seated near the back of the plane. Captain Diamond is blond, seven years younger than I, and likes to maintain the illusion of living in civilization by keeping her nails done and wearing mascara while on duty. Already tired of being alone, I wandered back through the curtain and found Captain Diamond.

"Hey, howya doing, Sue," she said. "Come on back and join the party."

In my mind flashed that scene from *Band of Brothers* where Lt. Buck Compton gets reprimanded as an officer for shooting craps with enlisted men because the two groups aren't supposed to mix socially. Captain Diamond wasn't an enlisted soldier, but it was clearly expected that I sit in first class with the other senior officers. Hunched next to Captain Diamond was a private, a big tall kid whose legs were already buckled underneath him. In a snap, I decided that this was his lucky day.

13

"Private," I said, "how would you like to swap seats with me? I'd like to sit next to my friend here."

"Ma'am, really, ma'am?" he gulped.

"Yeah," I said. "Up front in first class you can stretch out your long legs from here to Maine. Only one condition: you have to carry my flowers. There'll be an empty seat next to you—shouldn't be much of a problem."

His face broke into a huge grin. The private stood up, his head touching the ceiling. I'd estimate he was six feet, five inches tall.

One of the senior officers was checking something in the back of the plane and interrupted our plans: "Colonel—hey, that doesn't look good for us. You should be sitting in first class."

"What for?" I answered with a grin. "There's no booze allowed on this flight."

Everybody laughed. The senior officer shrugged. I guessed I had won over the backseat crowd. The private went forward. I sat down next to Captain Diamond.

About three hours later, we landed at Fort McCoy's sprawling grounds and were sent to the barracks where we'd be living for the next three months. Our quarters were old World War II–era barracks, pretty Spartan even for the military. As a base, Fort McCoy can be a pretty desolate place with its white-brick buildings, gray Wisconsin skies, and heavy surrounding woods. I was assigned to a room on the second floor.

A colonel is supposed to be in a room by herself, but suddenly I found again that I didn't want to leave my friends. I nosed around and discovered a room with three beds, one still vacant, and figured out a way to switch to that room. Things still weren't quite right: the joint needed a bit of sprucing up. I dug around for a pair of scissors, cut up the roses George had given me, and walked from room to room, scattering rose petals on each pillow.

Captain Diamond came with me and placed some mints on the pillows, too. A group of young women noticed what we were doing and asked why.

"Listen," I said, "I love the Ritz-Carlton. Whenever I'm there, they always put rose petals on my bed. I figured we could do the same here." Everybody laughed.

I'm glad we had a good laugh that first night. We knew those rose petals and mints would be the last bit of civilization we'd encounter for some time. The next three months at Fort McCoy would be some of the toughest training we'd ever do before flying to the heart of the battle in Iraq.

❖

CHAPTER 2

My Personal Toccoa

B Y THE GLOW of the dial on my watch I squinted at the time: 4:45 A.M. I had 15 more minutes. All was quiet in the old barracks. The two bunkmates in my room breathed steadily beneath their covers. I stared at the wood ceiling for a moment, then closed my eyes again.

I could see them. Taste them. A remarkable assortment of rich, bold reds. I'm not a huge drinker, but now and again I enjoy a flavorful wine with an evening's meal. I saw myself on a summer night with all our friends over at our house. Lit candles glowed in the background. I tilted a glass away from me and checked out the wine's color and clarity from the rim's edge to the middle of the glass, the first small sip sparkling on my tongue. Ahhhhh. A heavenly light-bodied finish.

Beep. Beep. Beep. Beep. The alarm clock pierced my dream. The army. Fort McCoy. Training. Iraq. Those were my current realities. There would be no wine tastings this summer.

I showered, dressed in a hurry, and headed out. Ahead was our unit's first full day of training. Coffee percolated in huge stainless-steel containers, and the smell of bacon mixed with the mustiness of the mess hall. I couldn't stomach heavy food that early in the day, so I opted for orange juice and Rice Krispies instead. My buddy Captain Diamond slid her tray next to mine as we sat on one of the old wooden benches.

"Ugh," she said, forking through her scrambled eggs in search of an edible bite. "I guess the army is feeding its soldiers pretty good these days, but I think you made the healthier choice with whatcha got there."

"Yeah," I said, laughing. "I figured I'd make this my own private spa experience. You know—lose weight, get tanned, train for Iraq." I reached for more juice.

"On your feet, soldiers!" came a shout from near the door. "Formation, on the double! Let's go! Hup! Hup! Hup!"

That was breakfast. We hupped outside into formation and stood at attention, all 450 of us in the unit. It must have rained the entire Wisconsin spring, because the mud sogged under my boots. Steam rose in the morning air and I glanced up into a cloudless sky. Moisture and heat: a dangerous summer weather combination. That day would prove to be sultry, particularly for early June. I wondered how hot things would become throughout the next three months of training.

A commander assigned us all into platoons with about 30 people in each. Captain Diamond and I were both placed in Echo Platoon. It felt reassuring to have a friend alongside me. I saw some other familiar faces, people I had come to know during our unit's weekend training sessions throughout the year, but there were plenty of strangers, too, as solo reservists had joined up with our unit from all over the country.

Captain Diamond and I stood shoulder to shoulder in the ranks. In spite of my higher status in the unit, I wasn't the officer leading the platoon. It didn't work that way for training. A junior officer was platoon leader. He received his orders from our commander, who was in charge of other platoons as well. Several of us had heard rumors that a good friend of ours might become our platoon's commander, but we had no such luck. The commander assigned to us came with a reputation. This rumor sent chills up and down our spines.

She stood before us with a brick face. Our new commander was short and thickly built, maybe 160 pounds, and her holstered revolver stuck out almost perpendicular to the ground as it poked out from her wide hip. For about two minutes, she seemed to stare straight through us. I wondered if there was something behind us that we hadn't seen. Slowly she took off her sunglasses, scraping the rims against her forehead in the process. Her dark-blond hair was pulled back in a severe bun. Everything about her seemed unbending and tight.

"Eyes on me!" she barked. "My rule is law, and you will obey it. From now on, whatever I say is the way things are. You will not question me. You will not complain. You will not roll your eyes. You will not sigh. You will simply obey. That is your only job. And if you don't like the way things are, then too bad."

Good grief, I thought. *Lighten up, Francis. This isn't the movies. We're all medical personnel here, not Green Berets.*

The first sergeant handed our commander a clipboard. She barked through a list of regulations, punctuating the end of each with a phrase we would all come to know too well in the near future: *If you don't like the way things are, then too bad.* She reminded me of Dirty Harry, the Clint Eastwood character who considers everyone a punk and invites them all to make his day. Regulations issued, our commander turned our platoon back over to the first sergeant, who motioned us to the supply depot for new gear. I glanced at the few soldiers on my right and left. Their eyebrows were lowered, their mouths forming frowns.

"Whew, she's a real piece of work," someone muttered behind

me as soon as our commander was out of earshot. "Can't believe that fatso is going to be grilling our asses all summer."

"She's certainly not what I signed up for," said another. "I'm a surgeon, for Pete's sake. If she keeps up with all that regular army crap, we'll need to take her down a peg before long."

Captain Diamond gave me a friendly swat on the shoulder as we marched to the depot. "So we've got a real Captain Sobel, eh?" she said, and rolled her eyes. "Fun summer, here we come."

Captain Sobel was the company commander who trained Easy Company at Camp Toccoa, as portrayed in *Band of Brothers*. History has registered him as a controversial figure. On the one hand, he succeeded in crafting a finely tuned fighting force of soldiers, and I know a lot of the E Company veterans feel that way about him. George met Captain Sobel's son, Mike, and they got along well. On the other hand, the series generally portrayed Captain Sobel as a screaming, inflexible jerk, and the name "Captain Sobel" in some military circles has become synonymous with bad commanders. Regardless of what Captain Sobel was like in real life, certainly there are people in today's army who act similar to how Captain Sobel was portrayed in the miniseries.

I feared for our "Commander Clint" (I preferred to think of her as the Clint Eastwood character) in the months ahead. It's not easy to be effective as a senior officer in charge of a medical reservist unit. We're army, sure, but we're not frontline infantrymen charging the enemy with our bayonets. A senior officer must know how to command respect, but if her unit is primarily made up of doctors, nurses, and other nonregular army personnel, she'll do it much more effectively if she first respects the professionals she's leading. A smile goes a long way in leading the reservist army. I hoped Commander Clint wasn't in for more than she bargained for.

The supply depot consisted of a long line of people getting fitted for equipment. As reservists, we had been previously issued the bulk of our standard military gear, but going to Iraq meant specific outfitting for combat situations. Our gear included a barracks bag, a duffel bag, a waterproof bag, a belt, two canteens, a tool kit, a first aid case, a field pack, an entrenching tool, a liner with poncho, a wet weather parka, a pair of wet-weather trousers, a sleeping mat, and a black sleeping bag. It seemed almost like a light list to me.

We were instructed to wear our new gear at all times from then on, including during training at Fort McCoy. This would be no shorts-and-T-shirt situation. Our new gear also included a bulky bulletproof flak jacket. When I picked it up, the jacket felt like almost 30 pounds of extra weight on my shoulders. For a moment I thought back to grade school, where I had really struggled with my weight. In eighth grade, I was pretty much the fattest kid in my class. I almost felt like that fat kid again, but this extra weight was designed to save my life. I strapped the flak jacket on.

For a weapon, I was assigned a 9 mm revolver. Most everyone else in my platoon was issued an M-16 rifle. That was okay; I didn't particularly want to carry a rifle. I didn't even want to stick a revolver under my belt, but I wasn't complaining to anyone just then. A soldier's weapon is meant to be carried at all times. It goes everywhere with you. "All," "everywhere"—those are big words when you're hefting around an extra ten pounds of loaded weapon in addition to the other gear you're already carting. Your rifle's supposed to be in your hands when you brush your teeth. It's snuggled up next to you when you hit the pillow at night. It rests next to you when you heat up meatloaf from a can while out on maneuvers. The last thing I wanted was to carry a rifle everywhere I went.

As I strapped the revolver into my holster, a little shiver ran down my spine. It's a difficult thing as a nurse to carry any sort of weapon. My profession is tasked with saving lives; weapons tend to take them. Someone brought up the same question to our sergeant. He shot us a dirty look like we were all stupid civilians, but then changed his tone and gave us a courteous answer. Normally, a medical unit would have military police officers (MPs) assigned to it, he explained, who would carry rifles and protect the medical staff. But things were different over in Iraq. If you were out in the compound, you needed to be able to take care of yourself. That included protecting a patient, if needed. This was a war zone. The real deal. Everyone, even nurses, needed to know how to be able to shoot—and kill—the bad guy.

My revolver came with a hard leather holster that fit around my hips. The holster felt bulky and cold in spite of the early-summer heat. I glanced self-consciously at my hips and wondered if my revolver stuck out perpendicular to the ground the same way Commander Clint's did. Fortunately, it rested next to my leg without too much tilt.

When the fitting was through, I found a few seconds to take a much-needed bathroom break. That extra cup of orange juice from breakfast was now sloshing through my bladder. In the stall, I found out firsthand the difficulties of wearing a revolver on your hip. Everything needs to get unbuckled in proper order to come down, revolver and all. Then your clean gun jangles on the mucky floor with heaven knows what kind of disgusting dirt. This would never do. After I washed my hands, I headed outside wondering how I was going learn to eat, sleep, and perform all bodily functions for the next year and a half with a revolver permanently strapped to my hip. Then I spotted the solution. A lieutenant colonel walked across the compound with a brown suede aftermarket holster strapped around his back and neck that fell at his side. "Hey, cool holster. Where'd you get that?" I asked.

He glanced over at the restroom then back to my hip holster. "Yep, we've all been there." He grinned, shaking his head. "My cousin makes these holsters. Real easy access. You wear it on your left so you can pull your revolver out with your right hand. Eighty bucks delivered. I'll order you one if you'd like."

I grinned back. "That's going to be a real lifesaver—thanks." A little helpful camaraderie goes a long way among the troops.

Lunch came next. We didn't go back to the mess hall. We ate on the grounds. It sounds like a picnic, but it wasn't. Lunch—that day and every other day during training—consisted of Meals, Ready-to-Eat (MREs). Think of MREs as soldiers' rations. It's the grub you eat in a foxhole. MREs are also known as:

- Meals Rejected by Everyone
- Meals Rarely Edible
- Meals Rejected even by the Enemy
- Meals Resembling Edibles
- Meals Ready to Excrete

When you're handed an MRE, you get the luck of the draw from a variety of dehydrated entrées such as chili with beans, veggie burgers, manicotti, and spaghetti. The entrée is meant to be heated with a flameless ration heater. You also get a side dish, salt and pepper, crackers and peanut butter, powdered beverage mix, a candy bar, and chewing gum, as well as matches, eating utensils, a napkin, and a moist towelette. I guess the quality of MREs has improved over the years, but the commonly held thought is that with every MRE you get three lies for the price of one—it's not a meal, it's not really ready, and you can't actually eat it.

"What you get in yours?" Captain Diamond asked.

"I tried not to look." I had already experienced the joy of MREs during weekend training sessions.

"I got frankfurters in mine, four of 'em all gummed up together. Four fingers of death, if you ask me."

"The crackers were pretty good," I said. "That's all I ate. You know how many calories are in these things?"

"Four thousand? Maybe five." Captain Diamond laughed wryly. "We soldiers on the go really need to pack it in."

I grinned back at her. "Yeah, something like that anyway."

After lunch came our first language class. An Iraqi civilian contractor put us through the paces. *Ben Amerikaliyim ve Turkce bilmiyorum. Benim size hicbir zararim dokunmaz,*" I repeated with the rest of the class. "I am an American. I do not speak your language." I figured those sentences would come in handy. In addition to learning phrases of the four languages we would encounter in Iraq—Arabic, Turkish, Persian (Farsi), and Kurdish—we received cultural awareness lessons. Alcohol is forbidden in an Islamic country. Polygamy is generally allowed.

Lectures comprised the rest of the afternoon. Dinner was back in the mess hall. More seminars came after dinner. We were back in our rooms at 9:00 P.M., the end of the first full day. I phoned George from my cell phone.

"How'd everything go?" he asked.

"Pretty good. But it was no wine tasting."

"What?"

"Promise me one thing, George. Sometime this summer, throw a wine-tasting party at our house. Make it a real big spread with all our friends."

"Well, sure, but you know I don't drink." (George is a teetotaler except for the occasional glass of champagne at a celebration.)

"Yeah, I know. Just do it for my sake, okay? It's really important to me. Take pictures. Imagine I'm there with you. Then tell me all the details of how the night went. I'll experience it all by proxy."

George laughed. "Well, Susan, you've got yourself a deal there."

THE NEXT MORNING we were up and running. Literally.

Commander Clint stood motionless, hands behind her back, her revolver poking sideways on her hip, and we headed out. She stayed put. Unlike other commanders, she decided not to run with us.

I hate to run. Pretty early into the exercise I had an ache in my side and was bringing up the rear in case I needed to make a quick exit into the woods. That army food was playing havoc with my insides. A mile passed. Then another. We kept going. My mouth felt dry. Sweat pooled under my helmet. My flak jacket bore into me and my revolver bounced on my hip. Weather reports called for near 100 percent humidity with temperatures in the 90s. This was no casual morning jog. The morning air felt thick and murky, and I wasn't sure if I could go any farther. Someone from near the end of the pack dared to grouse aloud about the heat. I didn't see who it was. "Well," panted Captain Diamond under her breath. She had circled around the end of the pack to where I was. "If you don't like the way things are, then too bad." She grinned.

Mercifully, the run came to an end. A few more seminars came after that. A few more calisthenics. Sit-ups. Push-ups. We ate our MREs out in the field. After lunch came the obstacle course. We crawled on our bellies around land mines, jumped up and over pits, shinnied our way over walls. You don't want to get captured.

Then we learned how to throw a grenade. I had a hard time with this. Six months earlier, during winter, while at a friend's house for dinner, I had slipped on an upturned rug at the top of some stairs, fallen on my shoulder, and torn my rotator cuff. Throwing a hand grenade feels a bit like throwing a baseball. Accuracy is stressed above any particular tossing technique, but basically you face sideways toward the enemy, remove the grenade's safety clip, grip the pineapple with your throwing hand while twisting out the safety pin, and arc the grenade at the bad guy. You hope it lands on or near him and blows him up. Then you hope he's brought to you so that you can patch him up, which is again the irony of being a nurse.

I chucked and I chucked. After an hour of practice throws my shoulder ached. My whole body felt sweaty and hot. I wished there were some shade nearby. The early-afternoon sun was unpitying. I took a sip from my canteen.

Suddenly, the guy next to me tapped me on the back and pointed. "Hey, isn't that your friend?" he said. "She's down." His eyes looked worried. He was a cook, not a medical professional. Our unit had its share of support personal assigned to it as well, including communications technicians, administrators, and drivers.

I looked down the line to where Captain Diamond had been tossing grenades. She was slumped in a sitting position on the ground, her face pale. Two or three others crouched around her. I ran over. She had vomited on the dirt and looked like she might pass out any second.

"You okay, Captain?" I said.

"Yeah, it's just this heat, I think," she said. Her skin felt clammy to the touch.

"How much have you had to drink today?"

"Oh, plenty. At least half a can of Diet Coke."

She was kidding, but we both knew that dehydration is no laughing matter. Captain Diamond was taken to the sick bay, where they chalked up her nausea to the heat. With all our physical exertion, we needed to drink about a liter of water per hour from our canteens. It required constant discipline to keep that much liquid flowing through us. Captain Diamond's wasn't an isolated case. The installation reported 18 heat casualties over the course of the day. Captain Diamond missed training for the rest of the day but came back strong for the next.

The third day we stormed a village. I don't know why a nurse would ever want to do this, but someone believed it was necessary for us to learn. We hiked out in the field to where a makeshift Iraqi village had been set up. People dressed like Iraqis milled about the structures. Someone was supposed to be invading the village, I think. We heard a *bang, bang, bang.* Gunshots. "Let's go! Let's go! Let's go!" our sergeant yelled. We ran to the village. Some of us secured the area. The rest looked for the wounded and treated whoever was found. The whole idea was to prepare us for absolutely anything we might encounter.

Next came weapons practice. When our turn came up, we were briefed on safety techniques first. The idea, said the instructor, is not to shoot yourself. You also don't want to shoot anyone you don't want to shoot. Sounded pretty basic.

To practice shooting, each of us stood on an open range with our weapons. When a marker came up some distance away, we had a moment to decide if it was something we needed to shoot at and, if so, to fire. We were graded on how closely we hit the intended target. Markers look like the heads and bodies of people. The heads were just generic heads—not specifically terrorists. Sometime in the next few weeks, we would get graded on our shooting. There were various levels—sharpshooter, marksman, and expert. We had to shoot 60 points out of 100 to pass, I think, and we had to pass the shooting exercise to pass training. Hoo boy! Seeing some of the doctors and nurses shooting in line next to me that first day on the range, I wasn't sure if any of us would ever make it to Iraq. Myself included.

"Seems to me we'd be more effective if these markers were a little bit bigger," said the doctor behind me.

"Yeah, make mine the size of a barn door," I said.

Shooting had two other components. The first of those was night shooting—basically, shooting markers in the dark. We went into the range in the evening and blasted away. The second was shooting for accuracy while wearing a gas mask. The gas mask was a piece of gear I had already had assigned to me for several years, so I had brought a mask over from my unit at Hanscom. I wear bifocals, so my mask is fitted with prescription lenses. A prescription gas mask—how's that for the latest in fashion wear, ladies?

When you first put on a gas mask, it's hard to breathe. Practice breathing through a straw for an hour while on a Stairmaster, and that will give you an idea of what it's like. The temperature heats up and you sweat inside the mask. When you take it off, you have marks on your face. It's also hard to hear; the volume drops when you shoot targets with a mask on. It's just you, your breathing, and the weapon banging away in front of you. Yeesh.

So that was shooting. Slowly, the days merged into one another. A week passed and then another. I was up at five o'clock each morning, then it was *go, go, go* until nine at night. Shower, sleep. Shower, sleep. Or sometimes for variety, sleep then shower, sleep then shower. Yep, life got really creative. Some days were less difficult than others, but nothing was what you would call easy. Near the start of training, I had purchased extra language tapes from the commissary, hoping to get ahead in language studies. I already spoke Portuguese and Spanish. Languages tend to come easily to me. But I didn't touch my tapes. No time. I had also bought a journal, thinking I'd write in that each night. It sat untouched in my barracks bag.

As the weeks wore on, we began to feel like soldiers more and more. We went on marches with weight in our rucksacks. Five-milers in the morning or evening. Captain Clint checked to make sure nobody cheated with the weight requirements in our packs. It always seemed like our platoon—and the other two platoons led by Captain Clint—were the first on the field in the morning and the last to go to bed at night. Other units were training at Fort McCoy along with us. We'd see them out marching, or talk to them in passing. "How are things going for you?" we'd say.

"Great, just great!" they'd say gleefully. "We just love training. It's so much fun"—or words to that effect. They were sincere, too. They loved their training. So why didn't we? My two bunkmates were both in other platoons. They also came back to the barracks at night and described great days. Other soldiers would get to go to San Antonio for specialized training. Some platoons got whole evenings off to socialize in the barracks or just kick back or whatever. That certainly wasn't our story in Echo Company. It was a long day every day, at least 5:00 A.M. to 9:00 P.M. Captain Clint was really putting us through the wringer.

When nearly a month had passed, it dawned on me that the date was July 2. I was sitting on my bunk after a hard day's training listening to my bunkmates talk about how much fun they were having, when I realized nothing had been planned to celebrate Independence Day. I'm often our unit's morale, welfare & recreation (MWR) officer, but at McCoy I had passed the duties over to a younger officer, Captain Mac, as everybody called her. Right then, Captain Mac sauntered into our room, a jaunty look in her eyes as always. "Hey there, Colonel, what're you drinking?" she said, and grabbed my glass out of my hand.

I let her take a few swigs before I answered, "Metamucil." It was no joke. That army food can really bind up a person.

Captain Mac gulped and handed me back the glass. "Well, hey, that's the best-tasting Chardonnay the army ever dished up," she said with a grin.

Suddenly a plan unfolded in front of my eyes. "Captain Mac," I said, "how soon can you get together a party-planning committee?"

"I dunno. Why does it matter? Captain Clint won't let us have any time off."

"Just leave that to me." I grabbed my cell phone and called George. "Hey, sweetie, how soon do you think you could ship those four boxes in our pantry over to McCoy? You know the ones I'm talking about? Overnight? You're a doll. Why do I need them? Well, I'll let you know if I can pull it off."

A colonel can be persuasive when she needs to be. Permission to hold an Independence Day celebration isn't too much of a hard sell for us patriotic types. Really, it didn't take much sweet talking at all. Our unit was granted permission to have the Fourth of July off—as long as we didn't leave the base. It was no matter to us. We were going to celebrate!

On the night of July 3, the package from George arrived. Captain Mac and I gathered the members of the party-planning committee and went to work. The next morning dawned hot. We trucked our supplies to a nearby park on the grounds of Fort McCoy and set up shop. By that afternoon, we had a big barbecue pit set up with hot dogs and hamburgers sizzling on the grill. Not an MRE in sight. Our platoon showed up soon after, their mouths watering. There was fresh potato salad and cold sodas, Jell-O, apple pie—all the food you'd expect at a Fourth of July celebration. Soldiers tossed Frisbees and joked around with a good-natured tug-of-war competition. A few guys smoked cigars as freely as golfers on a neighborhood fairway. We even had cold beer. There was a two-drink maximum, so nobody got snookered.

And we served wine.

Just a taste. We served it in the fancy glasses that George had overnighted us in the package he sent. We served a remarkable assortment of rich, bold reds. It felt like we were home again, the carryover from some kind of civilian dream. The friendly smell of backyard barbecue drifted all over the grounds of Fort McCoy. Soldiers kicked back, talking, laughing, unwinding. No one talked about terrorists or Iraq. We sounded like a bunch of neighbors gathered for a front-lawn tailgate party. Captain Clint stopped by; she didn't stay long, but the fact that she had showed up meant there was hope for her yet. A lot of hope. I tilted a glass away from me and checked out its color and clarity from the rim's edge to the middle of the glass. The first small sip sparkled on my tongue. Ahhhhh. A heavenly light-bodied finish. I had my summertime wine-tasting party at last.

JULY PASSED AND August came. Mornings were stifling. A dull, arid breeze blew most afternoons. Any grass dried out and became brown. The bulb of red mercury in the thermometer by the mess hall inched up and up.

Strangely enough, the heat succeeded in pressing us closer together. We had a common enemy now, one that wasn't yelling at us all the time. Our unit felt like it was becoming a real team. We were still nurses and doctors, yes, but a new kind of confidence coursed through our veins. We could run for miles without passing out. We could hike long distances with full packs. We could shimmy through obstacle courses with a gritty smile. Our hand-grenade tossing was getting more accurate. Our language skills were improving. *"Sizin halkiniza benden hicbir kotuluk gelmez,"* we chanted in class. "I bear no malice toward your people." We were looking, sounding, and feeling more like the real thing.

The army isn't known for telling anybody anything. Officers are often left in the dark as well, since rumors can run rampant on army bases. In some units there's almost a rumor of the day. Juicy ones, too. Rumors began to circulate that we might get to go home for a few days at the end of training before shipping out to Iraq. I liked the sound of that rumor. There was only one hitch—and we knew this for sure: if a reservist didn't pass her shooting training, she definitely wouldn't get to go home. Fortunately, I had passed my shooting fairly early on in the summer. My score wasn't great, but it was good enough.

Others in my platoon weren't proving as fortunate. One nurse from Ohio, who was also a major, struggled and struggled to pass her shoot. Time and time again she came back with the same news. No luck. "Major Ohio" couldn't shoot for anything. The problem might have been caginess from a lack of brawn. She was a good nurse and a fine major, but she was slight of build. The barrel of the M-16 she carried was nearly thicker than her arm, and the rifle's blast nearly blew her over each time she fired.

"Colonel Luz, what am I going to do?!" Major Ohio asked one day after a particularly horrific low score.

I saw her score and shook my head. "It looks like you're doing everything the instructors tell you to do," I said. "You just need to hit the targets, that's all."

"I've got to pass this thing. I've just got to." There was desperation in her voice. She wanted to succeed.

"Keep it up, Major," I said. "The summer's not over yet."

"Yeah, but we're heading out on maneuvers for two weeks, and I won't be able to practice then. After that I'll only have one more chance."

I nodded and gave her a little hug. I wouldn't say it out loud, but I was worried for her as well. She was far too good a nurse to get washed out this early in the game. For the time being, we'd have to put her fate on hold.

Going on maneuvers meant living in tents out in the woods for two weeks. After being bused to a remote section of the camp, we hiked the remaining distance to our destination. We set up hospital tents first, then our personal living tents, then went to work. The idea was to simulate a variety of situations we might encounter overseas. Each test was graded by national army evaluators. The pressure mounted. Some units were known to fail. We couldn't progress to Iraq unless we passed everything.

One of my first scenarios involved a man dressed as an Iraqi civilian. He stood at the front gate of our compound wanting medical help. The tendency in a case like this is to allow your compassion to take over and let someone in immediately; however, we were trained to take a few simple precautions that would benefit everybody inside. First, check to see if he's got any sort of improvised explosives strapped to him or on his person. Second, evaluate symptoms. I noticed the man was sweating profusely and complaining of diarrhea, vomiting, and muscle cramps. Not a good sign—probably cholera, a communicable disease that can bring down an entire unit. I refused the man permission to enter until he checked out okay first. That meant I passed the test correctly. So far, so good.

Another man was sent to me with a bad rash and boils all over his hands and face. He had leishmaniasis, a disease caused by sand flies. I had seen it in real life back when I was in the Peace Corps. Mostly a disease of the developing world, leishmaniasis is rarely known in the developed world; most of those rare cases involve troops who have been stationed away from their home countries in places like Saudi Arabia and Iraq. Part of the problem is due to bad sanitation and waste left uncollected in streets, allowing the parasite-spreading sand flies an environment they find favorable. I was looking forward to that one. Right.

Another section of the test involved all of us in action at once. The simulation was a bus accident caused from a roadside explosion. People were brought in dressed up with a variety of wounds. Bloody bandages. Legs blown off. Who would we take first? Why? Our unit handled the triage correctly and passed that section with flying colors.

Personally, I was drilled extensively on combat stress, as I hold an additional military occupational specialty (MOS) as a psychiatric nurse. A soldier came to me with signs of depression. A failing grade would have come from telling him to buck up. But did I check to see if he had ever previously been on medication for depression? Did he ever have thoughts of suicide? Each part of the testing was as real as the army could make it. The blood looked like real blood. The soldiers acting in each case stayed as true to the scenario as possible. In another case, a female soldier came in, saying she had been raped by another soldier. I pulled the curtains to give her privacy, and the doctor performed the exam. I held the patient's hand, wiping my eyes silently when she wasn't looking.

On a lighter note, we heard a lot of curious sounds in our tents at night. Scufflings. Scurryings. Nibblings. At the end of maneuvers, we discovered that a mouse had been living in my duffel bag. It had munched its way through shirts and undergarments and deposited its droppings as thanks for the stay.

I shook out the mouse droppings and laced up my boots for the hike back to the bus.

Maneuvers were over. I was glad.

IT WAS THE DAY before the finish. Training was light that last day, just a seminar or two on the schedule. Mostly it was packing up and saying good-bye. But Major Ohio still hadn't passed her shooting test. I spotted her in the breakfast line, her brow furrowed, and came closer to where she stood.

"You can do this," I said.

She shook her head. "No, I don't think so, Colonel. I'm done."

"You've still got one whole day left."

She shook her head again, her eyes lowered.

"Would it help if you had someone down at the range with you? We could cheer you on."

A faint glimmer crossed her eyes. She nodded.

"C'mon, then, let's get to work."

It was just after 6:00 A.M. on the last day of training when Major Ohio fired her first bullet. Her M-16 bucked and whooshed in her arms. The bullet missed its mark by a good ten inches. She pulled the trigger again. This one was still wide, but an inch closer. She kept firing. And missing. An hour went by. Then another. Slowly, a small group gathered. "You can do it, Major!" somebody yelled. "Just aim a bit more to the right next time." Lunchtime came. We broke out some MREs and stayed at the range. The major reloaded her rifle. Bullets zinged into the dirt, over treetops, anywhere but where they should go. Three o'clock came. Four o'clock. The crowd stayed with her. "Keep going, Major, you've almost got it!" someone else called. Dinnertime came and went. A few drifted back to the mess hall, but the bulk of us stayed. The major kept firing. The instructor kept checking her score. Seven o'clock came. Seven thirty. Eight was the absolute cutoff point. It was either succeed by then or go home trying.

As the sun began to set over the western sky, the major was down to her last rounds. I was pooped. I think we all were. It all depended on this one last series of shots. I watched the major's face closely. She looked at me, nodded, then looked back at her target. I think she closed her eyes. *Bang! Bang! Bang! Bang!* Her rifle smoked and went silent.

The instructor checked the target, a frown on his weary face. He had spent the whole day at the range as well. It was five minutes to eight o'clock. He cleared his throat. "Well," he said quietly, "your score's not great, Major. But you passed."

We all let out a loud whoop. We had done it as a team! Nothing was going to stop us now! In front of us lay six glorious days of leave time. We were all heading home.

WHEN I CAME HOME from McCoy, the first thing I did was go to my sister's house. They had a banner over the door that said, "Welcome Home, Susie." It was a big party. I went in and caught up with everybody I knew and loved, but it was a strange feeling being home for such a short time. Mostly I was anxious to get going. I had a focus I couldn't break. We were trained for the mission now. It was time to embark.

With two days left of leave, I drove over to the ocean to collect my thoughts. A good friend of mine, Elaine D'Antuono, lives on the waterfront. She's older than I am, a retired lieutenant colonel, and wouldn't be going on this mission, which I felt sad about. She's a real Goldie Hawn type—everybody loves her. They used to call her Private Benjamin, in fact. We sat on Elaine's porch overlooking the Sakonnet Bay and talked.

"You ready for this?" she asked.

"Absolutely," I answered.

"It's gonna be hard, you know."

"I know."

She looked at me more closely and waited a few minutes. "I mean really hard."

I didn't say anything.

In the distance, I saw a flock of Canada geese lift up over the water on their trip south. The September sun was warm in the sky still. Another season was fast approaching, and it felt like anything could happen.

I didn't answer because I knew Elaine was right.

ON SEPTEMBER 27, 2006, our unit met up again at Fort McCoy and we were given our permanent orders. It's mostly a formality; in the army, you don't move anywhere without a command. We soon boarded a plane and flew to Kuwait, the sovereign Arab emirate that borders Iraq on the south. We traveled aboard a commercial charter on a DC-10. Everyone in our unit had at least one weapon (sometimes two), but we were still prohibited from bringing on knives and liquids. Go figure. Troopers snapped good-natured pictures of themselves with M-16s and 9 mm pistols inside the cabin. Once in Kuwait, we, along with several thousand other troops, were stationed at Camp Doha. There would be little additional training in Kuwait; Camp Doha simply acted as a jumping-off point that bridged our transition from America to Iraq. We would be there only a week.

As we stepped off the plane, the dense heat of Kuwait's air immediately washed over us like a tsunami. And we had thought Wisconsin was hot. This must have been 110 degrees. We were assigned to big tents, 50 soldiers in each. The tents were air-conditioned. Thankfully. Part of this exercise was simply to help us get acclimatized to the Middle East. Fortunately, we were allowed to wear PT shorts and T-shirts while at Camp Doha. We could also make phone calls home anytime we needed. Captain Diamond and I found a beauty parlor on base, a tiny place run by Kuwaiti nationals, and had our nails done. One last chance at civilization. Why not?

Our only real training at Doha was the test-firing of our weapons. We climbed aboard buses and traveled out into the desert where the firing range was located. I got in a line with the other soldiers and blasted away. Everything worked. That was it. Test over. There was nothing left to do.

In the distance, I spotted a line of camels. They were off to the side of the range and in no danger of getting hit. I had never seen a camel in real life. Their sides were dry and dusty, and they looked over at us while chewing placidly, straw hanging out of their mouths. I thought of the flock of Canada geese I had seen from a distance while sitting on Elaine's porch overlooking the Sakonnet Bay. Surely I had realized this before, but it was while I was watching the camels that the truth of where we were and what we were about to do hit me anew. I wasn't in Rhode Island anymore. I was spitting distance away from a real-life, blood-and-guts war zone. This was the real deal and I was here—ready or not.

❖

CHAPTER 3

In the Line of Fire

ONE OF 92 PASSENGERS aboard a C-130 Hercules flying from Kuwait to northern Iraq, I fingered the rosary in my hand and recited the Gloria Patri. I couldn't look out the window. There were none. The only people who had windows were the pilots up front and the gunners in the rear. The massive four-engine turbo-prop I was riding in was built like a steel stomach and employed to transport large numbers of troops and equipment; it was not designed for those who easily feel claustrophobic.

Five C-130s were being used to transport half our unit and its gear to Mosul. The other half of our unit had been sent to another hospital in Tikrit. Our planes flew at intervals to steer clear of a mass attack. As we rumbled through the air, I glanced toward the back of the plane, where our cargo was stowed on pallets. The aft section of the C-130 opens like a gaping mouth. You can hoist a utility helicopter into the plane if you need to, or drive a jeep aboard. My unit's gear formed an uneasily secured mound of duffel bags and medical containers. There are no overhead bins inside a C-130. No stewardesses offering peanuts and seltzer. Inside, the plane looked like an empty hangar. The metal jump seat gritted against the underside of my uniform where I sat against a wall. Whenever we hit an air pocket, my Kevlar helmet clacked against the metal side of the plane. I focused on the back of the helmet of the person in front of me and tried to take deep breaths. I tried not to think about how much I hated to fly.

It never used to bother me. Once I was fearless. Back in 1977, I was flying to Paraguay in the middle of a hurricane. Our plane slid across the runway, and we all bailed out the emergency chute. That's when I first questioned the safety of air travel. A little experience can erode the strongest of bravados. And it only got worse—on another occasion, returning to Rhode Island after two weeks of reserve training in Texas, the plane I was on plunged, leveled off, then started doing monstrous, unexplained dips. We were told later all engines had blown out except one. A couple of the New England Patriots were on board, hulking football play-ers with thigh-sized necks. The player next to me kept pawing at the thick gold rope around his neck; he grew so antsy he yanked it right off. Whenever I get nervous, I start to talk as quickly as possible—it doesn't matter to whom. I was wearing a brand-new outfit that I had bought to look good for George when I landed. It was an Anne Taylor herringbone suit with a short jacket and skirt. I looked so cute. I had a marvelous tan after being in the Texas sun for two weeks. On the first plunge, I spilled tomato juice all over my new clothes. I clenched my teeth, then opened my mouth: "Say the Hail Mary!" I called out. "Everyone! Pray! Now!" *Hail, Mary, full of grace, the Lord is with thee; blessed art thou among women, and blessed is the fruit of thy womb, Jesus.* We rattled off the prayer: football players, businessmen, mothers with small children—everyone around me followed my lead. When the plane finally touched down in Rhode Island, everyone erupted in long applause. Today, I fly only when I have to. I hate it, but I force myself to do it.

"Colonel!" The C-130 pilot's voice interrupted my thoughts.

"Colonel! We're almost in Mosul. Come to the top and have a look around."

I nodded and unbuckled my seat belt. His invitation was standard procedure. I'm sure it's more of a courtesy than anything. The pilot invites the highest-ranking officer up top to check things out. The flight crew sees everything you see, though undoubtedly better because they're used to looking out the cockpit's windows. Still, it's protocol for a military officer to be asked to survey the scene. I followed the pilot to the front of the plane, climbed a short staircase, and entered the cabin. The pilot resumed his seat. A copilot sat on the other side. A crewman with binoculars scanned the space in front of us, searching for flashes of gunfire. "So far, so good, Colonel," said the crewman with binoculars. "Everything looks pretty calm today. But you never can tell."

I couldn't help but notice that, from the air, Mosul looks a bit like Los Angeles on a dry day. Streets and rooftops stretch out haphazardly in dusty grids. Fields are brown and waterless. Roads are paved, mostly. Cars choke the main streets. As Iraq's second largest city after Baghdad, Mosul has a population today of about 2.6 million. I wondered what it had looked like thousands of years ago when it was called Nineveh, the city that God ordered Jonah to preach against because of its corruption. I remembered that the ancient citizens repented and the city was spared. From the cockpit, I could see the green-black shimmer of the Tigris River. I saw one of Saddam Hussein's old palaces. I saw the minarets of a dozen mosques. Many buildings looked bombed and crumbling.

Our destination was the Mosul International Airport, located on the west side of the Tigris. The airfield had first been occupied by U.S. troops in 2003 and had become a logistics hub for the military. Two U.S. military bases, Camp Diamondback and Camp Marez, were located next to the airfield. At any one time, about 17,000 troops and 10,000 civilian contractors manned the two bases. Our unit was heading for Diamondback. We'd been warned that the bases were surrounded by unfriendly folks. Rocket and mortar rounds from nearby insurgents were frequent. A year earlier, 24 people had been killed when mortar rounds struck a mess tent where soldiers had just sat down for lunch. A short time after that, 72 personnel had been wounded in an attack carried out by a suicide bomber wearing an explosive vest and the uniform of the Iraqi security services. Mosul was a city of heavy guerrilla activity. For the American military in 2006, it was considered one of the most dangerous places in Iraq.

"We're all set to land," said the pilot. "You want to stay up here with us?"

"Um, everything looks secure," I said. "I think I'll head back to my seat." We had been briefed on how we would be landing at Mosul, and I didn't want to chuck my cookies. No sooner had I buckled my seat belt than the plane took a sharp nosedive, then zigged and zagged, coming in crooked, trying to dodge any rockets that might be coming toward us. I let out a sharp gasp when I heard the wheels squeal on the tarmac.

"Go! Go! Go!" yelled First Sergeant Shirley Martino. A first sergeant is a company commander's right hand; he or she organizes the unit. Everybody looked up to First Sergeant Martino. She stood by the door, hustling troops out. We knew the orders: When the plane lands you run—you don't walk. You grab your gear, hurry after the person ahead of you, and sprint across the tarmac to the bunkers at the sides of the runway. This was a war zone. The only welcoming committee we'd ever see could be comprised of insurgents hiding near the runway, ready to blow our heads off with submachine guns.

I sprinted over the tarmac to a bunker. Made of cement with

sandbags on top, each bunker held about 20 troops. So far, no shooting. It was almost too quiet. I knew that near the airstrip was the infamous house where Saddam's two sons, Uday and Qusay Hussein, had been killed in a four-hour shoot-out with U.S. troops in 2003. Uday, the older and considered the more brutal of the two, had been Saddam's heir. Through my uneasy mind ran his résumé of extreme violent behavior: murder, torture, and rape. Uday's alleged crimes were as notorious as his father's. One example: As head of the Iraqi Olympic Committee, Uday allegedly oversaw the imprisonment and torture of Iraqi athletes deemed not to have performed up to expectations. Widespread reports said that Uday directed torturers to cane the soles of soccer players' feet to break their bones and end their livelihoods. He made athletes kick concrete walls until their feet broke. Sometimes he tied up poor-performing athletes and dragged them through gravel pits until bloodied, then immersed them in sewage tanks to induce infection in the wounds. I find it hard to believe that some people today can ever forget which regime has always been the real enemy of the Iraqi people.

We formed up at the bunkers, although not in "formation," and headed inside the base. When we heard the coast was clear, we breathed easier and shook the adrenaline out of our shoulders. Everything was quick work. An officer handed us the keys to our contained housing units (CHUs), and we were off. CHUs look like tiny trailers. Here on base, I had a CHU to myself. For once, I was okay with being alone. I figured some privacy would come as a welcome relief in a place of such intensity.

So that was it. We were there.

Funny. So quiet. Too quiet. There wasn't much else to do that first day in Iraq except settle in. Orientation would start at six the next morning. We had expected much more resistance upon our arrival. It had been explained to us that the 101st Airborne had been fighting in the surrounding city for a year and was getting ready to pull out. Another combat unit, the 4th Brigade, 1st Cavalry, was replacing the 101st. We were to become the hospital support for the new combat unit. Reports showed that whenever the U.S. military made such transitions, Iraqi insurgents escalated the violence. Mortar attacks became more frequent to greet the newcomers, not less. So why was our arrival greeted by such calm?

That night in my CHU, I lay on my bunk, thinking. My mind flashed back to a question I had pondered when I first joined the military some 23 years earlier. At the swearing-in ceremony at the Army Reserve Center in Providence, Rhode Island, I raised my right hand alongside the other new recruits and pledged to serve my country. Even as I committed myself, I wondered if the army had a place for people like me. You think of nurses in war zones as the blood-and-guts-type medical personnel, the ones with their arms elbow-deep in people's chests. But my job as a public health nurse mainly consisted of things like giving shots and holding sanitation seminars. I think one thing that interested recruiters about me was my additional certification as a psychiatric nurse. One of my responsibilities would be to help soldiers with emotional trauma. When the going got tough, I'd be there to help. Many people don't realize the stress soldiers go through. In the old days, nobody wanted to admit that soldiers ever went through emotional difficulties, even if they were regularly seeing people maimed or killed by bullets and bombs.

The scene from 23 years ago that flashed into my mind so vividly was this: a mentor at the swearing-in ceremony looked me in the eye and said, "Susan, if you ever go to war, you're going to be one of the busiest people there."

For a moment, I wondered if I was having a dream, but the

memory was so vivid I knew I was still awake. It was about two hours after sunset. I lay on my bunk, thoughts racing. The Islamic call to prayer could be heard, the fifth and final of the day. A beautiful yet eerily haunting sound, it warbled over a neighborhood loudspeaker. After that came silence.

I WOKE THE NEXT morning to another prayer call. Dawn in Mosul, Iraq. I lay for a moment, savoring the sounds of being far from home. I understood deeply that we were not at war with this culture. These people were not our enemies. The majority of neighbors who lived around our base were friendly, even welcoming the coalition's presence. Our enemies were the motley assortment of sectarian groups spread through the country who attacked coalition forces and even their own countrymen.

Captain Diamond met me at breakfast. "Sleep okay?" she asked.

"Like I was at the Ritz."

"Not me. I tossed and turned all night," she said. "When do you think this war's going to be over?"

"Not soon enough," I said.

Captain Diamond and I small-talked over our food, but I was listening with only one ear. In my mind I was sorting through what I knew about the war, trying to pinpoint a better answer to her question—for my sake as well as hers. I knew the initial objectives of the Iraq War had been accomplished quite quickly. When the war started in March 2003, the goal was to end Saddam Hussein's regime, capture and drive out terrorists, and assist Iraq in creating a government that would not stomp on the people all the time. Baghdad and the Iraqi military fell in April 2003, ending Saddam's 24-year rule of terror. On May 1, President George W. Bush had given a speech on an aircraft carrier under a banner that read "Mission Accomplished."

But new problems came after Iraq's government and military were destroyed. A new Iraqi government was soon created, but at least a dozen major insurgent organizations (comprised of more than 40 distinct groups) rose up to oppose the new Iraqi government and the coalition troops in Iraq. These groups' interests were driven by a variety of beliefs and grievances. They warred with one another as much as they warred against coalition forces. Three years later, that's why our troops were still here: to bring order from chaos.

"Hey, you still sleeping?" Captain Diamond's voice interrupted my thoughts.

"What?"

"I asked you if you wanted another cup of coffee."

"Oh sure, thanks," I said. "Yeah."

"What do you think we'll see today?"

"Could be anything, really." I shrugged.

"Yeah, that's what I'm afraid of."

I drank the extra cup of coffee Captain Diamond poured for me, thinking through again what I had learned about the objectives of our particular mission: The main coalition combat unit on our base, the 4th Brigade, was specifically tasked with a variety of missions, mostly going from house to house in Mosul to ferret out insurgents. The work had already proved dangerous and often bloody. Insurgents fight using guerrilla tactics, including mortars, missiles, suicide bombers, improvised explosive devices, car bombs, rocket-propelled grenades, and snipers using small arms such as assault rifles. The specific mission of our unit, the 399th Combat Support Hospital, was to provide medical support to soldiers and civilians wounded in insurgent attacks. In other words, we were the medical unit stationed with a frontline combat brigade.

Except there was no front line in Iraq. Not really. We were *on* the front line, or we were *behind* the front line. The line between enemies was blurred all around us. Like Captain Diamond had suggested, the only thing certain was uncertainty itself.

THE ORDERS I UNDERTOOK that morning, my first on base, were to report to the hospital where I and my specialist—a sweetheart of a young woman named Elizabeth Tice, in her early 20s—would meet our counterparts, the duo we'd be replacing. Public health (my job) and preventive medicine (Specialist Tice's job) always go hand in hand. Our specific task is to keep healthy soldiers from getting sick. It's a lonely role. Of the 27,000 soldiers and civilian contractors on the two bases, Specialist Tice and I would be the only ones with this job.

Everything looked fairly routine inside the hospital that first day. The base hospital itself was not huge, just 32 beds total, but it was thoroughly modern and well equipped. A few wounded civilians and Iraqi soldiers occupied beds, but most were empty. What I noticed mostly was how crowded everything was because of all the orientation going on. Personnel from the new and old teams fell all over each other as they described techniques, asked questions, and scribbled notes. The army refers to the two groups involved in this type of orientation as Right Seat/Left Seat. The Right Seat shows the Left Seat what's been happening. Then the Right Seat leaves and the Left Seat owns the hospital. As members of the Left Seat, we needed to absorb everything very quickly. The Right Seat would soon be gone, and we would be left to run the joint on our own.

Major Heidi Kelly greeted me in the specialty clinic. Private First Class Tara Edminston was by her side. I liked both of them immediately. Major Kelly was in her early 30s, attractive, with a husband in active duty and a young son and daughter back home in Fort Lewis, Washington. She was the public health nurse I would replace. PFC Edminston was cute, tiny, maybe 105 pounds soaking wet. In her early 20s, she kept her long brown hair tied up loosely on the back of her head. Specialist Tice would replace her.

"Okay, Colonel," said Major Kelly, "let's start at the beginning."

"You know, it really is okay," I said. "You can just call me Susan."

Major Kelly gulped and smiled quickly. Few military people are used to informality in senior officers. "Uh, sure, Colonel, um, ma'am . . . Susan," she said, then whispered, "I was a captain until just recently. I only just became a major."

I smiled. "You're doing great, Major. I'm sure we'll get along just fine."

Major Kelly showed how she had been giving a series of tuberculosis injections and flu injections inside the clinic and out in the community. PFC Edminston explained how she had been testing water on base and doing inspections of safety techniques for food. They walked us around the hospital, then took us on a jeep tour of Diamondback and Marez bases. Diamondback is fairly small even for a large-scale overseas base. You could walk across the base in about half an hour. Even so, there's everything you could want on base, including a PX for groceries, a mess hall, a small movie theater, a beauty shop, and a bank of phone booths. Diamondback reminded me of a little overseas village. There were more trees than I expected for a desert climate. The temperature was only in the low 90s, not bad at all.

We spent all that day, then the next, then the next in orientation. From sunup to sundown, Specialist Tice and I shadowed Major Kelly and PFC Edminston, going over all that we'd need to learn. They secured an armed escort and a Humvee, then took us on a more large-scale tour around the bases. Everything looked very quiet and calm. We met with an American veterinarian vaccinating cows against wild coyotes—just business as usual. As time wore on, Major Kelly and PFC Edminston both started to relax and began calling me Colonel Susan. PFC Edminston told us all about her boyfriend, a combat medic also on base. They were getting really serious, she said with a smile, maybe planning to get married soon.

By dinnertime on the fourth day, orientation was becoming routine. Before long we'd grasp all we needed. Just before 6:00 P.M., we finished our last session of the day. "See you at dinner," said Major Kelly and PFC Edminston in unison. It got hot in the early evenings, so Major Kelly was heading back to her CHU to change into PT shorts for dinner. PFC Edminston wanted to spend a few minutes with her boyfriend. We all agreed to meet up again at dinner.

The base felt sleepy in the late-afternoon sun. Hospital beds were all empty by now. Bees buzzed around a tiny date palm tree that someone had planted by our housing units. I glanced at my watch. From outside the base, a prayer call began to sound, a bit earlier than usual this evening, I thought. Then it finished.

Silence.

Absolute silence.

I walked inside my CHU and dropped off my bag with all the books and notes. In a second I was outside again. The mess hall was a five-minute walk away. I glanced across the quad to where the big American flag waved in the Iraqi sun.

Busy? I thought. *If this is what it means to be busy, I could get used to this.*

The overhead speaker crackled. I felt the hair on the back of my neck rise. I'm one of those ultraintuitive individuals—almost like *M*A*S*H*'s Radar O'Reilly, who heard choppers before anyone else could.

The command from the speaker came terse and urgent: "Bunkers! Bunkers!"

When the first mortar hissed in and landed with a crash, I didn't think to feel fear. It was more a sense of incredulity: I couldn't believe that somebody actually wanted to kill me. What had I done to anyone? More mortars came in a heartbeat. Bombs flew into the compound and exploded, again and again. I covered my ears. Everything around me turned to fireballs and smoke and rocks and noise. All around me people were running and diving and yelling and cursing. My feet felt stuck in the sand. The mortars sounded like a traffic jam full of cars simultaneously backfiring: *Kaboom! Kaboom! Kaboom!*

A sergeant I didn't know shoved me toward a bunker. "Move!" he yelled. "Run!" I ran and slid inside as the ground continued to shake. A lot of people were already in the bunker. I moved toward the end of the group. You can't stand up inside a bunker; you just crouch. Through an open area, I could see a lot of mortars hitting the airfield. Many looked like they were hitting the dining hall—the place where I had just been headed.

I heard footsteps rush toward our bunker. Breathless, a soldier slid into the opening. "Any QRF in here?" he said. "Enemies at the gate. Rest of you lock and load." One soldier in our bunker nodded and followed the other soldier out, running toward the base's entrance to counter whatever insurgents were trying to get in. Every unit has a QRF—quick reactionary force—usually comprised of the strongest young combat soldiers in the group. I wasn't too worried about insurgents entering our base. Our guys would make quick work of that. Nevertheless, I pulled out a clip of bullets and locked it in place in my revolver. Normally you don't keep your weapon loaded on base unless there's a threat. "Lock and load" is the command to be ready for anything.

Almost as one, three messages flew over the loudspeaker. The voice of the loudspeaker is always an intelligence officer, a member of the 24-hour surveillance team who can see bombs come over the radar. The first message was "all clear." I felt my adrenaline spike down slightly. The second was "100 percent accountability," meaning everyone needed to report to the hospital to be counted. The third made me tremble: "MASCAL!"—code for mass casualties. This is the first time I had ever heard it for real. The message meant that a lot of soldiers and civilians had been seriously wounded; it was a command for everyone to fly.

In a second we were all out of the bunker, sprinting toward the hospital. I wondered if another mortar attack would hit us on the run. I headed for the specialty clinic to report in. I made it to the ward, let the person in charge know I was alive, and threw on a hospital top and a pair of gloves. It's not unusual to get covered in blood in an emergency. I had seen a lot of gore before, but thoughts kept running through my mind: "Will I be able to handle this? Do I have what it takes to not fold?" I set up a stretcher. Then another. My specific job during any MASCAL is to take care of the expectants, the people not expected to make it. My role is to be the last person they see—to administer morphine and dress their wounds, to soothe them into eternity. People would be brought to me to die.

A woman burst through the door. I heard her tears before I saw who was making them. The woman's shape had a familiar look. She ran closer. "PFC Edminston's been hit," she said. It was Major Kelly. "It's Tara. She got it really bad."

In a moment of crisis all formalities are dropped. "Tara's going to be okay," I said and held the major close. "It's in God's hands.

Pray with me, Heidi—pray." At that moment neither of us knew how bad PFC Edminston was. We chose to believe the best.

"Why now?" Major Kelly said through sobs. "We've been here a whole year. Why today? We were just about ready to go home."

I steered her toward a nearby chair and helped her sit. "Tara needs you to be strong for her," I said. "You can do this."

Bit by bit, the story came out. The young PFC was near the dining hall when mortars hit. Insurgents knew most troops would be in the mess hall that time of the day and specifically targeted that area, seeking the most damage. PFC Edminston took shrapnel in the stomach. It tore her up pretty good. Her boyfriend carried her to the hospital. He sprinted the whole way, throwing his back out in the process. I wish I knew his name. Had it not been for his actions, PFC Edminston would not even stand a chance. At least now there was a slim one. PFC Edminston was in surgery almost immediately.

A friend of Major Kelly's came in and stayed with her. There was more work to be done. As a senior officer, I had access to all areas of the hospital. I left for the ER to see what types of injuries were coming in. Everything was hustle and bustle for some time. In the emergency room, doctors and nurses treated more people who had been hit by the mortars' flying metal and glass. Rows of wounded were waiting to get into surgery. Small puddles of blood dotted the tile.

A young soldier sat near the door, his leg bandaged around the shin. His eyes wore a vacant look. He rested his M-16 on his knee. I guessed him to be about 19.

"You okay, Private?" I asked. He stared at me a moment too long before he remembered himself.

"Ma'am, yes—yes, ma'am," he said. "Not too many colonels talk to me."

"What happened to your leg?" I asked.

"Aw, it's nothing, ma'am. He glanced at the bandage. "Probably just bone chips, they think. They're going to cast it as soon as they get a spare minute." He looked away.

"You need anything to eat or drink?" I asked. "You hungry? You probably didn't get any dinner tonight."

He shook his head, repositioned the rifle on his knee, then covered his eyes with his free hand. I sat down beside him. "What's going on?" I said.

The soldier sat saying nothing. As tough as he was, he was crying. "My buddy got it really bad, ma'am," he said. "He's just going in for surgery right now. . ." His voice trailed off.

I put my arm around him, rubbing his shoulders, then thought for a moment. "If I can get you in, you want to see him before his surgery?"

He looked up. "You can do that?"

I located the guy's buddy in pre-op and asked the doctor if he minded allowing some goodwill to be brought to the troops. Scrounging a wheelchair, I helped the soldier in and wheeled him over to where his buddy lay on a bed. "We've only got a minute or two," I said. "He may not be able to hear you, but speak to him anyway. Let him know he's going to be okay."

The soldier's buddy had already received a sedative; his eyes were closed. I could see he had lacerations around the face and left shoulder. Blood soaked through a bandage on his arm. His jaw looked crooked, probably broken.

"Hey, man, it's me," the private said. "If you can hear me, give me a thumbs up." The wounded man's hands remained still.

"He'll be okay," I said, moving to push the wheelchair away. "Doctors will do everything they can."

"No—wait, please," said the private. He pulled himself closer to his friend and positioned himself next to his friend's ear. The private leaned over and breathed it as a whisper: "You stay with me. You hear that? You stay with me—you're going to live." His words bore the slightest hint of a command.

That image guided my tasks for the rest of the night. There were no expectants on that fourth night of our orientation. Not then. All the wounded were somehow willed to live. Periodically, I checked on Major Kelly as she waited for PFC Edminston to come out of surgery. Mostly I went from soldier to soldier, asking if there was anything anybody needed. Water? Something to eat? Somebody to talk to?

PFC Tara Edminston came out of surgery around midnight. She lay unconscious in the intensive care unit and was set to be shipped out to a recovery hospital in Germany the next morning. Nobody was allowed in to see her just yet, but she was going to make it. Doctors told Major Kelly to come back in the morning and be the first person PFC Edminston saw.

By 3:00 A.M. the line of wounded had been all taken care of. My next shift began at 7:00 A.M. I decided to return to my CHU for a few hours' sleep. "Help us, God," I prayed as I lay down and tried to close my eyes. "Surely there is more to come." I wasn't concerned anymore that I would be able to do my job. Strangely, I wasn't afraid of dying either. I had survived other tragedies in my life. I believed that God had a purpose for keeping me alive during those times. I knew I had a job to do in Iraq. My work in this war zone had officially begun.

❖

PART TWO

How I Came to Iraq

CHAPTER 4

To Become an Army Nurse

N OBODY WHO CHOOSES to go to war goes there overnight. By
the time I went to Iraq, I had shed much of my youthful
naïveté as the result of a number of shaping experiences along my
life's journey. Yet at the beginning of that journey, I confess that
much of what consumed my mind was food. At least it did one
particular Friday night in late September 1968. I was a freshman
in the nursing program at the University of Rhode Island, and
the cafeteria was serving steak.

"Gee, Sue, you've got a real appetite tonight," one of my dorm
mates said. She was sitting next to me, nibbling a salad, twirling
her long blond hair with one finger. The girl glanced at the pile
on my plate. "Did you go jogging before dinner or something?"

I laughed. "Ha. That's a good one. Pass me the bread, will ya."

She took a sip of lemon water, apparently thinking. "Say, a
bunch of us are heading over to the student union building later
on. You want to go with us?" She tossed her long hair with a
smile. I think her father owned a ski resort in Massachusetts, or
maybe a diet pill factory.

"Nah, lots of studying to do. Thanks, though." My mouth
was full.

She was beautiful and thin and blond, my dorm mate. And

did I mention tall? Almost as tall as my other dorm mate, who was equally beautiful and thin and blond. They wouldn't be around long. They would both be snapped up by sororities soon. This was first semester and the rush wasn't on yet, but they would have no problem getting accepted. My dorm mates were the types of Barbie girls that sororities go gaga over, girls made for lipstick and tight sweaters and cute skirts and hot days at the beach. Me? I didn't see a sorority in my future anytime soon. Sororities weren't interested in fat girls.

I headed back to the serving trays for another plate of steak. I was already stuffed but figured I might work up an appetite again while studying. Another steak and a couple slices of bread would make the perfect sandwich for later on. The juices seeped into the folded napkins as I tucked the package under my arm. Taking food out of the caf was against rules, but it wasn't hard to smuggle some anyway. I made it out unseen. The difficulty came as I sprinted back to my dorm room in Barlow Hall, excited that snack time wasn't far ahead. *Yaaaaaaa*. What was that? I tripped in the grass. Slid maybe. The steak fell out of its napkin, almost in slow motion, and I pawed at the air as the meat spiraled like a football and plopped some distance ahead on the grass. Was anybody looking? I dusted off the steak and gave it a kiss for good luck. Hey, I'm Irish! The steak was still good.

Through the closed door of my dorm room I could hear the open and shut of banging doors down the hall. Kids were talking and laughing and heading out on the town. The fuzz-laden sounds of a Jimmy Hendrix solo pounded from a stereo a few rooms away. A faint whiff of marijuana smoke drifted through the air. I sighed. I didn't want the party life. Not really. There were coffee stains on my open notebook. That's what I did for a social life. Drank coffee in my room. Secretly ate leftover steak. And doughnuts. And ice cream: chocolate, strawberry, vanilla, fudge ripple, pecan praline. I loved thick, swirly ice cream. There were no boys in my life. No crushes. Not much going on at all. Friends, sure, but we were mostly the studying types. Except I wasn't even sure how to study. Not really. College was proving a whole lot harder than high school ever had been. I laid out my clean pajamas, shimmied out of my clothes, wrapped a towel around myself, and stepped on the scales. One hundred and sixty pounds. I had already gained ten pounds since the start of school, packed on my five foot four frame. Not exactly sorority material. Tugging on my pajamas, I closed my textbooks and fired up a hot plate to reheat the steak. Yep, I was really changing the world now.

I had never wanted to go to the University of Rhode Island (URI). Not at first, that is. I wanted to go to New York's Columbia University, the Ivy League school where my world-changing mother's cousin, both nun and nurse, had gone. But my parents, Patrick and Margaret Corry, couldn't afford Columbia, so that meant going to URI. Fortunately for me, URI was no slouch of a school when it came to their nursing program. It had made several top-ten lists for nursing schools nationally. The professors were tough and dedicated. They knew we all came in with skulls full of mush. Their goal, as they saw it, was to transform us into dedicated professionals.

Some professors took harder lines than others. Dr. DeWolf taught zoology, one of the core classes for the nursing program. In his class we dissected cats, frogs, whatever we could cut up while learning about bones, blood, and the body. Dr. DeWolf kept a residence on campus that we passed every day on the way to class. Kids called it the Wolf Den. We considered him mean. A real howling wolf. We studied as hard as we could, all of us, or at least we groused about needing to study while we ate our ice cream sundaes. When the grades came back at the end of the semester, I found that I'd flunked zoology. In fact, nearly the whole class had flunked. Dr. DeWolf had even flunked his own daughter—she wasn't in our class, but that's how the story went. I think three kids in the class passed. The rest of us were mush skulls.

I was devastated. Flunking a class meant I needed to make it up in summer school. Truly, I wanted to be a nurse. That's all I had ever dreamed of doing. The nursing program at URI was a five-year program, but I had figured if I took classes during summers, makeup courses notwithstanding, then I could graduate in four years. I hadn't expected that to be too hard. Maybe I hadn't thought it through—what was there to think about? I had been too busy wondering about things, worrying about things, blowing things off to eat or go through the study motions or hang out with girlfriends. But that F in zoology woke me up and got me started on the road to more serious thinking. I resolved to truly buckle down and hit the books. That thought of becoming a nurse consumed me, guided me, spurred me on. To become an army nurse—that goal unswervingly held my focus.

Summer school is where I first met Donna Manion. She wore a hip brown corduroy jumper that fell above her knees, a jazzy white long-sleeved blouse, and a jaunty scarf at the back of her hair. Her earrings jangled whenever she moved her head. Donna was tall but a bit chubby like me. She had an easy smile and a quick laugh, and we soon became best friends. Donna, too, had flunked zoology, and she joked that we first met over a bag of bones. We had actually met a few years back, but we didn't remember each other. She had gone to a rival high school, and we had probably seen each other around at district events. Donna and I became study mates. We buckled down and learned how to absorb the material so that it stuck in our brains. I made honors after that.

Besides studying seriously, Donna and I had tons of fun together. One day in a nursing class, about five minutes before the class started, I was sitting near the back joking with other girls. Suddenly, the whole class became deathly quiet. The professor, Ms. Harrison, was looking straight at me, my mouth still flapping. "Okay, Miss Corry," she said, "whenever you're finished, we'll begin."

I wished the chair would swallow me alive, but at least I had the resolve to think quickly. "Oh, I was just telling these girls around me how great your class is."

The professor squinted then slowly grinned. "All right, then, Miss Corry," she said. I never made a peep from then on.

Donna and I were in chemistry lab one day, when I needed to use the women's room. I mean really! But the nearest women's room was on the other side of campus. There was a men's room nearby. "Donna," I said, "you stand guard. I'm going in." When I came out, there was a male professor standing next to Donna, tapping his foot. He scowled. "Oh, was this the men's room?" I asked. "I forgot my glasses and couldn't read the sign." Donna and I giggled all the way back to class.

The nursing program wasn't designed to accommodate social lives. Prospective nurses left the campus daily at 6:00 A.M. and weren't home until dinnertime, often later. Many of our classes were held off-site at the hospital or in practicum situations that involved hands-on learning. Each semester we were required to take one practicum, but the medical-surgical practicum lasted more than one semester. We were required to wear white stockings, polished shoes, and a starched nurse's hat. The uniform was a big deal back then. Our instructor implied that if your shoes weren't polished, you were a horrible nurse. I hated all the technical stuff, drawing blood, whatever. For a moment or two I toyed with changing programs.

Two other practicums saved me: psychology and public health. I loved psych. I liked caring for people; that's what nursing was all about for me. We could choose where we wanted to go for the psych practicum. I chose to work at the Institute of Mental Health. Many of the wards were locked, but I never felt scared. Being around the patients reminded me of my aunt Ellen, wheelchair-bound and mentally handicapped, who had lived in our house while I was growing up. For my public health practicum I went to South Providence, the projects, the worst area of Rhode Island. We went to schools, visited clinics, made house visits, worked with families. Donna was afraid to go to that area, which is funny because today Donna works in a school in this same inner city. B.J., a black friend of ours, took the practicum with me. In my naïveté I thought I was perfectly safe with B.J. beside me.

"What are you talking about?" she said. "I can get robbed or shot the same as you."

As I mentioned earlier, I still had a lot to learn about thinking things through. Fortunately, B.J. and I never had any problems during our public health practicum. Still today, we're the best of buddies.

Those experiences at the Institute of Mental Health and in the projects renewed my passion for nursing. I stayed in the program with new resolve to become an army nurse. I figured I could go to Vietnam and save a life. It wasn't that I couldn't save lives in a stateside hospital, but I held a romantic image in my mind of nursing in an overseas war zone.

There were plenty of students across the United States who were thinking. There was a lot of unrest on campus around that time. Civil rights demonstrations. Antiwar demonstrations. I was very sympathetic to the civil rights demonstrations because I felt that everybody was equal, but I differed from those who opposed the war. My father had served in World War II. We were a military family, and that was the standard that guided me. How dare anybody question the U.S. military? I wasn't watching much news. Richard Nixon was elected president in 1968 on a promise to end the conflict in Vietnam. About a year later, we heard fuzzy reports of a tragedy that had happened in March 1968 in a village called My Lai. Some reporters called it a massacre of innocents; some said American soldiers were just following orders. It was all confusing to me. There was a lot of debate, a lot of angry talk. If the bigwigs in Washington couldn't figure it all out, then how was anyone else expected to? The first lottery draft drawing—the first since 1942—was held in 1969. Many young men started saying they couldn't stand the thought of being drafted to fight a war they opposed. Then, in 1970, Cambodia was invaded. On May 4 of that year, the Kent State shootings happened and college campuses erupted around the country. I just kept studying. Donna's first cousin wore a hippie headband and always went against the establishment. But I just hunkered down to do what I was supposed to do. I never cut class. I never smoked dope. I never participated in a sit-in. I figured that since my parents were paying for college, I needed to buckle down, get good grades, and get through. That was all that was going through my mind.

I kept eating, too.

When you hang around a lot of girls in the evenings, you tend to eat a lot of snacks—pizza, cookies, chips, candy. No boys. No crushes. No dates. My junior year, my father let me have the family Rambler to drive. It became our floor's snack machine. On weekends I took my friends to my aunt's house to make cookies. Weeknights, all of us piled into the Rambler in our pajamas on a mad quest for ice cream. Once I ran out of gas and a policeman stopped to ask if we were okay. Yeah, just out for ice cream, we said. There were no drug checks for us. No being frisked. The policeman took one look at us, laughed, and called a tow truck. That was our life. One evening back in my dorm room, I shimmied out of my clothes, wrapped a towel around myself, and stood on the scales. A hundred and eighty pounds. Could that be right? How was I ever going to get into the army now?

My new resolve was to lose weight. I dieted and lost weight, snacked and gained it back, dieted some more, studied and studied, dieted and snacked, and didn't think much about what was happening in Vietnam, except that I wanted to serve over there and save lives.

Those were the activities and thoughts I focused on in college.

AS GRADUATION NEARED, I was back down to 150 pounds. I needed to be at that weight for my meeting with the army recruiter. Thoughts of becoming an army nurse consumed me now. I was certain that my destiny was to save the lives of soldiers in Vietnam.

During my last year in school, five of us—Donna, B.J., Linda, Nancy, and I—lived off campus in a little house on Scarborough Beach, right next to the water. We never had time to actually go to the beach, not to sun-tan or throw a Frisbee. Anyway, none of us were beach girls. Well, maybe B.J.; she was cool at whatever she did. Our house was located "down the line," as they said, where all the parties raged, but we never had any parties at our house. My sister had gone to URI just ahead of me and lived down the line her senior year. She was skinny and smart, and she had parties. Lots of them. She was free and laughed, and guys liked her. She was an English major and didn't need to study much, and she wasn't concerned with saving the world, at least not that she ever vocalized to me. Sometimes, after I closed my textbooks late at night, I gazed longingly at the refrigerator, holding on to my resolve to diet even as my stomach rumbled, and admitted I wanted to be like my sister. In all ways.

A few days before I was to see the army recruiter, it dawned on me that I should get my parents' permission first. I didn't really need their permission, not legally. It was more their blessing I was after. I figured that because of where my dad had been, that blessing would come readily.

I came home to my parents' house one day around Christmas. My mother began the conversation. "So, Sue, your last semester is ahead. What are you going to do then? Apply to the Rhode Island hospitals?" It was what most nursing students were doing.

"Well, actually . . ." I chose my moment of opportunity. "I want to be an army nurse and go to Vietnam."

"You are not going to Vietnam!" my father said. He was a man of few words. There was extraordinary firmness to his voice.

I hesitated, blinking a few times. I looked around the kitchen at the familiar chrome toaster, the telephone, the Formica on the kitchen counter. Didn't he know this was my dream?

"Why not?" I said quietly.

"That's not why we put you through nursing school. You're not joining the army. You're not going to Vietnam."

It was the absolute end of the discussion. I knew from the tone of his voice that he had put his foot down. I couldn't understand why a man who had served his country in the army didn't want me to follow his footsteps, but we were not big on discussing and hashing through things. I was not likely to get an explanation from him. My problem now was this: I had been pushing myself through college for four and a half years with one ambition in mind, and with just a few words from my father, that ambition had been crushed. What was I going to do next?

After I went back to school, I took a rare walk behind our house on Scarborough Beach early the next morning. Seagulls rioted over my head. All around me were waves and surf and driftwood and aloneness. As I walked on the sand I thought, really thought, for once. As much as I was able, I did the hard work of wrestling with ideas, motives, possibilities.

My only conclusion that morning was that I didn't know why my father had said no. I simply didn't know. I didn't know that my father, Patrick Corry—the man who had fought under General George S. Patton in the snow and muck at the Battle of the Bulge and who had earned a Purple Heart for being wounded and a Silver Star for bravery, who never showed us the medals or talked about the war to Mom or any of us kids—this man chose his method of coping for a reason. I didn't know then that my father had seen nurses die in World War II, and I didn't know that he was thinking he didn't want that to happen to his own daughter. I didn't know that he had been watching the nightly news closely, seeing the villagers with terrible burns, the toe poppers and bouncing betties (types of land mines), the intricate system of now-blown tunnels in the Than Khe area south of Chu Lai, the destroyed rice paddies, the soldiers without arms or legs, the kid with his mouth open and teeth broken and black bruises under his swollen left eye where he'd been shot, the lice and the ringworm and the paddy algae and the malaria and the dysentery, the demonstrators at home chanting and urging the country—our country—to hate our soldiers. I didn't know that my father could remember hearing the explosions from his own war, seeing the fresh bodies, smelling the blood as it clotted on necks and lay pooled in upper chest cavities. I didn't know that even after a hot shower, scrubbing as hard as he could, he felt that the stink was always there, the stink of what had been around him, the dense, greasy smell of the lubricant that he used to clean his rifle, the rifle that he had fired earlier in the cold, wintry days of war.

I gained this understanding only years later. The complexity had not yet been formed in my perspective. That morning walking the Scarborough Beach, there was simply a chubby young Catholic schoolgirl, nearly graduated from college, who was still growing up wanting to do something important with her life. She couldn't stand the thought of somebody suffering when she could do something about it, and she thought she was keenly aware of the presence of evil but really had little idea of its presence or power.

But my father knew something about evil.

"Watch out for those cowboys, Sue," he'd said when I hugged him good-bye the evening before. From the time we were little, he'd said that to me and my siblings whenever we went out the door. It meant "be careful." It was his way of showing love.

I wasn't mad at my father. He wasn't mad at me. And though I didn't know what to do next, I trusted him. That was one good thing I had going for me; I believe still today that my father had my best interests in mind, even if I didn't fully understand all his ways.

A PAGE OF MY LIFE quickly turned. If I couldn't go to Vietnam, then I needed to do something else to save the world. I convinced my good friend Donna Manion to join the Peace Corps with me instead of the army. I had always loved President John F. Kennedy, who had formed the Peace Corps years earlier. His stalwart words coursed through my mind time after time: *Ask not what your country can do for you . . .*

Donna's parents were upset with her decision. They feared for her safety. But my parents were happy that at least I wasn't going to war.

Donna and I both graduated from URI in May 1972. Her parents and mine gave us a trip to the recently opened Disney World as our graduation present. We planned to spend four glorious days in Florida over a long weekend. Upon our return, we'd take our nursing boards, the exams that would give us the RN designation in addition to our bachelor's degrees. We had been studying so much that we were confident we would pass. After taking our boards, we would head for New Orleans for our staging period with the Peace Corps, then board a plane for Brazil at the end of June.

While we were at Disney World, a huge tropical storm formed in the southern Atlantic Ocean, fed itself on moisture and heat, and whipped up violent winds and waves, rains and floods. The hurricane surged onto land and brought with it the heavy weather that damaged buildings, trees, and cars. Donna could be a bit of a nervous Nellie. She stayed up all night in our hotel room worried about the storm, worried about our upcoming exams, worried if we were going to make it back to college in time to take our boards. If we couldn't take our exams, we couldn't go to the Peace Corps. We'd have to wait until next fall to retake the test.

I thought being in a hurricane was exciting. They closed Disney World. We couldn't fly out of the airport and had to wait a couple extra days. I was feeling confident, though. The storm didn't harm us. For now, we were safe.

I couldn't imagine that there would be any more storms on our horizon. I don't think the possibility even crossed my mind.

CHAPTER 5

The Massacre of the Innocents

DOCTOR SUZANA, THEY called me—the children, even some of the medical staff in the tiny clinic in Quixadá, Brazil. Everyone in the town knew the American nurse who had come to help in their tiny hospital. Most of the national nurses in the hospital were actually nurses' aides, girls out of school a year or two with little or no formal training who helped out around the hospital, so a real nurse seemed as good as a doctor to them.

The family with whom I billeted in Quixadá consisted of a father, a mother, and three children. I hardly remember anymore what the mother looked like, nor can I recall the faces of two of the children. I've even forgotten their first names. But the father, a doctor, had a kind face with sharp eyebrows and a bushy mustache—I can see him clearly still. And the oldest son, Javier, was ten and had a dark crop of hair that flopped over on his forehead and a sweet, serious smile. And he could run. That was the first thing he announced when I met him. "Watch me run, Doctor Suzana," he said in Portuguese, and then padded off on his bare feet, spun around a hundred yards down the dirt road and barreled back, hardly panting, a triumph in his eyes.

"*Muito bem!*" I said. "*Prazer em conhece-lo, Javier.*" ("Good job. Nice to meet you, Javier.")

We became quick friends, Javier and I. If ever I had a free hour, he walked with me to the market where the road was paved, about a mile away, and we looked at the donkeys, pigs, horses, chickens, cows, baskets, and blankets, all the while practicing phrases in Portuguese, him schooling me, me soaking it in.

Three months earlier, Donna and I had flown to New Orleans for three days of orientation with the Peace Corps, and then on to Fortaleza, Brazil, the capital of the state of Ceará, for 12 weeks of training before heading out on our missions. The three initial training days in New Orleans were like nothing I had ever experienced before. I was excited by the city's blues and jazz; its boiled crawfish, jambalaya, oysters on the half shell; and its distinctive, almost Brooklynese dialect. We were introduced to about 50 other volunteers from all over the country. Most were just like us, recently graduated and eager for adventure. One, though, was a free-spirited girl with long hair parted down the middle; she talked nonchalantly about being on birth control pills. I remarked to Donna later that she and I had been really sheltered in college. Sure, we knew kids who partied and slept around, but birth control was never on our minds. We just wanted to be nurses and get through our training so we could serve our country.

We all stayed in a hotel in New Orleans. Donna and I roomed together. They held get-togethers for us on Bourbon Street. Nothing was very intense. We all knew that when we got to our various assigned countries we'd need to buckle down there. For Donna and me, it still felt like we were celebrating graduation at Disney World. The past four years had been so study-intensive. This was a break. Studying, yes, but a far more social time than college ever was for us.

The longer training session in Fortaleza was equally fun, but more intense. We stayed in a hostel there, not a hotel. Our lodgings were primitive. Mice scampered through our clothes and hair when we slept, and we had to keep our suitcases locked. The showers were cold, and the days started early and ended late. But it didn't feel difficult. I enjoyed my introduction to Portuguese: the raised vowels, the smooth romantic way the language rolled off my tongue.

Fortaleza is a modern city with a population of several million people. For three months, we marveled at the skyscrapers and beaches and omnipresent churches and dense humidity and unvarying tropical winds. We studied what it meant to go into a community of a different culture and help develop it, how to lend a hand medically in various situations, and how to begin to communicate in Portuguese, the language spoken by nearly all of Brazil's people. Peace Corps officials told us that any amount of language orientation we received in training would be limited: to truly learn and be effective, we needed to get ourselves into our specific jobs as quickly as possible and immerse ourselves in the culture, language, people, and task.

Fortaleza was where I met Doug. He was from out West somewhere, tall and blondish with a cool 70s mustache, handsome in a quiet, shy way. Doug seemed to like me, too, or at least didn't mind practicing his Portuguese phrases with me as much as possible. Within a few days, we were all hanging around together—Donna and I, Doug, and his friend DeWayne, a bearded too-tall cowboy who fell madly in love with Donna within moments of being introduced. DeWayne professed his undying affection to her within the hour, intense and sincere, and offered her a ring and a house and a picket fence in Texas with everything a woman could want—kids, golden retriever, milk cows—the whole farm was hers. But DeWayne was a hick from the sticks, Donna whispered to me in private. They would never make a match.

Doug, on the other hand, was the real deal. He came from a ranching background similar to DeWayne's and had also studied agriculture, but he was no hick. Doug's work with the Peace Corps would help people learn new farming techniques, new ways of planting and irrigating that would grow hardy crops and sustain lives. I respected him for wanting to do that. At night, back in my room with the mice scurrying around, I dreamed that one day something special would happen between Doug and me. When I thought about Doug, I got giddy, breathless almost, like I wanted him to give me a big squeeze and I'd squeeze him back and neither of us would let go for a long, long time.

As part of our training in Fortaleza, we were instructed to go out into the community to practice our language skills. We needed to go into restaurants and order food in Portuguese, into department stores and buy shirts or socks—that type of thing. One day while the four of us were coming down the escalator in a department store, I stepped off too soon, fell, and bumped my leg. Doug was right behind me and came up quick with his eyes full of concern. "Sue? Hey, are you okay?" he asked.

No, Doug. I wanted to say. I'm not okay. In fact, you need to take me in your arms and give me mouth-to-mouth resuscitation. But I didn't say that, of course, and right away we were all laughing about my tripping.

"Hey, Sue, weren't you the one who wanted to be a nun back in high school?" Donna asked me one evening after I confessed my true feelings to her about Doug. "How's this feel now?"

I thought for a minute. Doug truly was my first crush. I wanted something more with him. I wanted to be his girlfriend, maybe even his wife. This was something new I was feeling, something wild and uncontrollable and exciting and calm all at the same time, something I thought only pretty girls ever felt.

"Well, I . . . I don't want to be a nun anymore," I said. "That's for sure." I then threw my pillow at Donna.

It was great to have Donna with me in Fortaleza. Most people went into the Peace Corps alone. Donna felt like family. But when our training in Fortaleza was up, we needed to part company. In those days, they sent all volunteers out individually, even single women. The Peace Corps figured that since there was so much need in the world that we would all be more effective if we went by ourselves. We were more spread out that way; there were more of us to go around.

It was September 1972 when we completed the training. On our last day in Fortaleza we all posed for group pictures outside the hostel. About six kids stood in front with their instant cameras and snapped away at the rest of the group, who were sitting on the steps. Doug sat in the front row. He was wearing a red shirt, shorts, and sandals; his legs were tanned, and he had a faraway look in his eyes. Maybe he was thinking about his upcoming Peace Corps mission, but maybe he was also thinking about something different, some sort of future with me. Oh, I hoped. I sat in the back row with my hair feathered. It was about 90 degrees outside, and on the sun-baked steps in front of the hostel the glare was directly on us. For once, I wore a short-sleeved shirt. Somehow with Doug in the picture, I felt okay enough about myself to bare my arms. Maybe having a crush changes things like that. You feel all these new possibilities. Most of the group was set to meet up again in a few months for our first break. There were no phones where any of us were going in the meantime, but we all promised to write letters to one another. A lot of hope can be written into a letter.

It took 12 hours for me, alone in the country for the first time, to travel by bus from Fortaleza to Quixadá. People sat or stood all over the bus. Wares were piled high on the roof. The rickety old bus belched smoke and broke down several times along the way. From time to time, it would make unannounced stops to let people get off and stretch their legs or buy coffee or food from vendors by the side of the road. I ate anything the vendors sold without thought of getting sick. Cornmeal wrapped in leaves soon proved a favorite. I tried a drink made of avocado, milk, and sugar, and liked it. Big hunks of fried cheese and eggs were a popular fast-food offering. Kids ran up to me at every stop to say hello and examine a white person up close. I felt like a celebrity.

Ahead of me lay two years of immersion in the day-to-day ebb and flow of a rural village. The Peace Corps was classified as a government job and, for my services, I was paid 11 cents per hour, which I would collect in a stipend at the end of my two years. Money was no one's motivation in the Peace Corps; we just wanted the adventure of serving. You needed to be settled into a profession already to be in the Peace Corps. Nurses, doctors, teachers, and people with agricultural degrees tended to do well. My specific job was to help out in the hospital in Quixadá, as well as to set up small health clinics, miniposts we called them, in outlying towns. To set up each minipost, I needed to secure supplies such as vaccines, simple medications, and bandages; line up ambulances (usually a jeep); and teach nurses' aides how to assist doctors in their responsibilities. Teaching hygiene, health, child care, and English to people in the town was also part of my job.

Stepping into Quixadá at the end of the long bus ride felt like walking into an 1880s village. I imagined seeing pioneers—Portuguese-looking characters from *Little House on the Prairie*—walking up to say hello. But mostly the town was filled with men in slacks and button-down shirts; women in dresses and head coverings or in jeans; kids running, playing, laughing, squabbling; and cows, donkeys, and chickens. And more chickens. Everywhere underfoot there were chickens.

Quixadá is in the interior section of Brazil. Mountainous rocks border the town. I spotted a river nearby with a bridge and a huge rock that looked like a sitting hen. The town itself was mostly made up of adobe houses with white walls and black gaping holes for windows; no glass, only shutters. There was a movie theater in town that consisted of a cement building with one of those home-projector slide show screens set up in front. There was also a bus station that provided infrequent and slow service; a train station that ran on roughly the same schedule; a few clubs that offered loud, exuberant music; a tiny post office (where I'd pick up letters from Doug); and the marketplace—row after row of everything Quixadá had to offer. Including the outlying areas in the hills, some 10,000 people called Quixadá home, so maybe it wasn't that small after all. It just seemed small after coming from the large cityscape of Fortaleza.

Within a day of being in Quixadá, I bought a bike. Most people there traveled either by bike or by donkey. Riding a bike was okay by me. I had vowed years ago that my life's work would never involve sitting at a desk or being in a classroom if I could help it. I wanted to talk to people, help them, be on the go, up and around—that picture held the most promise to me.

The house where I stayed was nicer than most of the others in town. Even so, the doctor who owned it seemed to make very little money. It was a cement-block house, and there was no running water. You heated water on the stove and had to go to the backyard to take a shower. But it was more convenient just to use cold water. There were no beds in the house; everyone slept in hammocks. There were glass windows, but we still all slept under mosquito nets at night.

My days started at 6:00 A.M. at the main clinic, which served as our base. The clinic had an emergency room, a few hospital beds, and a couple of wards. People went to the clinic only for serious stuff, since most had no money for routine care. Someone had to have at least appendicitis to warrant the expense of being treated at the clinic. Babies were born at home with the help of midwives, although women usually did come to the clinic if they needed a cesarean section. A heart attack victim was usually shipped to Fortaleza. There were some rich people in town who could afford to have heart attacks. Their houses were located on the village outskirts, where they sat on more land. There was no middle class. People were either rich or poor. Because I was a white person, I was considered rich. And, even making 11 cents an hour, I truly was rich by comparison. I ate three times a day and would fly home to America at the end of two years. By Quixadá standards, that meant I was wealthy.

When the work at the clinic was running smoothly, we began to make forays to outlying villages to set up the miniposts. Early the first morning, the doctor and I loaded up rice, beans, vaccines, and bandages in the jeep and started to head out. The jeep's engine made a sad grinding sound. A puff of smoke blew out from under the hood.

"So what do we do now?" I asked the doctor.

He grinned and climbed out. "We ride."

He didn't mean bicycle. He meant donkey. As the weeks passed, I learned that donkeys broke down far less often than the doctor's jeep. Sometimes it took two or three hours to reach our destinations, even when the jeep was working. We often brought a local dentist with us. About all he did was pull teeth. Any and all medical supplies were in short supply, so if people got a Tylenol and a tooth pull from the dentist, they considered themselves fortunate.

Whenever we arrived, we set up a clinic in the middle of a village and word would spread. Sometimes people already knew we were coming. They lined up for hours in the blazing sun to see the doctor. I was appalled at the diseases I saw—leprosy, dysentery, malaria, trypanosomiasis, leishmaniasis, dengue, measles, fungal infections. There were also people infected with lice, people with unhealed wounds and open sores, mothers with 15 children and no milk, stooped elderly people with rickets—and they all stood in the blazing sun with their diseases, tears, flies, and hope.

The forays to outlying villages were normally just day trips, but occasionally we traveled far enough that we needed to spend the night and come back the next day. Or sometimes we purposely set up a clinic for several days at a time. For overnight trips, we took our own hammocks. Once I forgot mine and had to sleep in someone else's hammock, someone who lived in the village. A couple of days later, my head began to itch. I scratched and scratched and chalked it up to the heat, but the itching continued. I seldom took hot showers, but back at the doctor's house I heated up a bucket on the stove and shampooed my head really well. The itching continued. Not only was my head itching now, but my eyes were starting to bug me. Maybe I had picked up an eye infection somewhere. I itched and itched and rubbed my eyes and tried to figure out what was wrong. A nurse's aide knew the problem.

"Doctor Suzana, the only thing that will help is Kwell," she said in Portuguese.

Kwell was a powerful shampoo that contained the insecticide lindane. A few years after my stay in Brazil, it was linked to a variety of health problems and banned in many countries, but back then it's all we had, so I washed my hair with Kwell and hot water. Then I cut my hair short as an additional precaution against future infestations of lice.

But that wasn't the worst. My eyes continued to itch. Not my eyebrows, but my eyelashes. Again the nurse's aide knew the problem. I had lice in my eyelashes. Kwell was too toxic to be used so close to someone's eyes. There was only one solution. The nurse's aide nodded her head. I sat back in a chair, gripped the armrests, and tried to close my eyes. I could see the tweezers coming toward me. My eyelids snapped back each time she yanked. One by one she pulled out my eyelashes. I bawled and bellowed; tears ran down my face. "Please, no go berserk on me, Doctor Suzana," she said. I composed myself and whimpered as she finished up.

As painful as my lice infestation and its cure was, something much more painful happened within my first few months in Quixadá. Sometime around November, the medical team was staying overnight in a community out in the hills. There were seven other people besides me, the doctor, another nurse, a few nurses' aides, the dentist, and the driver. We went to bed late as usual; I think we were staying in a school. It was not yet sunrise when screams in Portuguese jolted the early morning air. *Come! Come! Doctor, come!* The screams were frantic. Desperate. I couldn't understand all that was being screamed. A man was shaking us, still groggy in our sleep, screaming for us to follow him quickly.

We shook the sleep from our eyes and ran after the man. We usually wore to bed whatever we had worn the day before. He led us only a short distance to an adobe house, the home of a poor family in the village. The doctor, dentist, and our driver went into the house right away. They motioned for us, the women, to stay at the door, but the other Brazilian women went in anyway. I thought maybe I had heard the instruction wrong, or not quite understood. It was a small house, so I stayed outside. There was more wailing inside, a sort of gasped, shocked sound. It sounded like it was coming from some of our team. I shifted my weight onto one foot, then the other, then decided to go in. Maybe I could help. Wasn't that why I was here in the first place?

I saw the mother of the family first. I made the same gasping shocked sound I'd heard the others make. Something stuck to my shoes; it felt like I was standing in paint. It was blood. The floor was covered in it. She had been pregnant. Her belly had been slashed open, and the baby had been removed by force and had died. There were three rooms in the house. I walked to another. The father was there, dead. He, too, had been slashed. I don't remember exactly how many children there were, but they were all dead in the third room, all hacked by a machete. Some of the kids still lay in their hammocks. They must have been killed while sleeping. In the big room, the simple furniture looked disarrayed. A struggle must have ensued there. There was nothing we could do. The whole family was gone.

Dawn was just breaking. Bits and pieces of the gruesome story trickled in. A cousin, most likely insane, had used a machete to murder everyone in the family. Machetes were common throughout the region. People used them to open coconuts, to chop down trees and brush. You'd see people walking down roads swinging their machetes. There was no apparent motivation for the slaughter. In the end, eight people were dead.

Talk was running through the village about lynching the cousin, a young man. They had tracked him down, and he was in custody nearby. I saw him quivering under his ropes. He looked delusional, his eyes wide and glassy. He was covered in blood. Someone said he had confessed to what he had done.

A short time later, we found out that one young boy had survived. He was maybe two years old. A neighbor sat holding the little boy on her lap, trying to comfort him. He might not have known all that had happened, which was a good thing. When the attack had taken place, his mother had probably tried to hide him. I walked over to the little boy, crouched down to his level, and put my hand on his arm lightly. He didn't turn away, so I stroked his arm and looked into his eyes. He was crying, inconsolable. What would his future look like? What would he remember of this horrible day? The murderer took more than just the little boy's family. He massacred the little boy's innocence.

When the cleanup started, we went about our regular business for the day. There was nothing more we could do. We were already there in the village, and it would not have done anybody any good if the doctor had left early. So we saw patients and gave shots and did whatever we normally did. I think more people than usual stood in line that day because word was spread farther that we were there.

I'm not sure if I wrote Doug about the experience or not. We were writing quite a lot just then, as often as we could. Not romantic letters, but just folksy, chatty ones, talking about our experiences, our adventures, our grand plans to save the world. Sometimes I wondered what it would be like to kiss Doug. I had never kissed a boy, not really. Another girl in the Peace Corps might have talked about her birth control pills nonchalantly, but I was still a virgin.

ON MY FIRST CHRISTMAS away from home, another picture was taken. I took the picture this time, so I'm not in it. The picture shows the center of Quixadá, the town where I stayed alone as a single woman. The sun is out, and there is no snow for Christmas, not in Brazil. The sky is blue and a tree in the background is Kodachrome green.

Some Peace Corp friends are in the picture. We met up again for Christmas in Quixadá after being apart for three months doing our specific missions. There's Donna with her long hair; Steve with his bushy beard; Chris, another nurse; and another guy also named Steve, a geologist. A little Brazilian boy wandered into the picture. He's looking at the camera with his hand on one hip a little distance away from us. All of us friends had been at a fiesta the night before and are wearing these crazy wide-brimmed hats. Doug and another volunteer named Tim were off somewhere in town when the picture was snapped, but they came back soon. My film was all used up by then, so I didn't get a picture of Doug. I sent the picture I took of my Peace Corps friends back home to my parents, writing on the back, "All of us here are really close." I was still smarting from the slaughter I had witnessed, but I wanted to write home about something that felt normal.

Brazil is a Catholic country, so I attended Mass with the rest of Quixadá on Christmas day. I don't remember if my other friends came to Mass with me, although I know Donna did. The linen corporal was spread over the center of the altar, and the communion bread was placed on a paten and the wine in a chalice. "Blessed be God forever," the priest said as he washed his hands in purity. I felt the bread and wine go past my lips and onto my tongue and become part of me, the mysterious body and blood of Christ. I thought about Christmas, the birth of Jesus, and how familiar and comforting my memories were of carolers and Christmas trees, presents and hot chocolate, Santa Claus and "Jingle Bells," even though I was so far from home. Surely, I had heard the story from St. Matthew's Gospel told a hundred times before, but for some reason that morning, another part of the Christmas story replayed in my mind and wouldn't leave. Perhaps I was still thinking about the murder in the village. It was hard to shake those memories.

Snippets of Holy Scripture came to me. Images flashed in my

mind—Renaissance paintings I must have seen in high school Western civilization classes or maybe during confirmation classes when I was 12. Shortly after Jesus' birth, King Herod grappled with a question posed by the magi who had traveled to Bethlehem looking for a newborn king. "Where is he that is born king of the Jews?" The question proved too much for Herod. No one was going to be king except him, so he ordered an execution of all the baby boys in Bethlehem. One after another after another, the infant males were slaughtered.

The entire gruesome incident is known throughout modern history as the Massacre of the Innocents. Giotto painted the incident, as did Rubens—in Rubens's painting, big fleshy nude soldiers are seizing the male babies of Bethlehem and dashing their heads against the base of a column. Wailing women are being held back, terror written on their faces, horrified at the brutality. I remember hating to look at those paintings when I saw them in school.

"*Ite, missa est.*" The priest concluded the Mass in Latin.

"Thanks be to God," we responded in unison. The priest walked out and the people around me got ready to leave. I was still wrestling inwardly. Donna gave me a nudge. "Sue—you okay? What's eating you?" she said.

"Yeah, yeah, I'm fine." I chewed my bottom lip.

Christmas. Murder. Those two opposing thoughts continued to mix. The Massacre of the Innocents was part of the extended Christmas story, but I couldn't figure out why. Jesus was born and a bunch of boy babies died. Why, I wondered, didn't we ever hear the full story? Christ came to bring peace on earth. Hope for mankind. He's the gentle and wise shepherd who cares for the little lost lambs. I tried to hold on to these kinder, gentler images, fighting the other details that wouldn't leave.

Donna and I walked out of the church into the hot Brazilian sun. Then part of the fog in my spirit seemed to drift away. I didn't grasp the full implications yet, even as I juggled the various pieces in my mind. But I glimpsed this: If the world was actually all that nice, as I had always imagined, then Christ would not have needed to come to it in the first place. That's why the two stories—the birth of Jesus and the Massacre of the Innocents—were so closely linked. To truly follow in the footsteps of Christ's mission, like I was trying to do, meant you also needed to understand and face the reality of evil.

They're gone now, those questions of my youth. They have been partly answered, passed over. The slaughter of the family happened in November. Then it was December and Christmas. Then it was January 1973. I still had a year and a half to go in Brazil to complete my commitment to the Peace Corps. Then there was more pain.

JAVIER AND I were walking to the market in January. It was Saturday morning; the daylight came to us broad and clear, and people were up and around. We were going down the street to buy cheese, get eggs, I don't remember exactly what. Javier was running mostly, as much as he could, while I walked. He ran around me and ahead of me and came back and took my hand for a few steps, then darted away. The boy was always running. *"A minha disciplina favorita é matemática,"* he said on one of his return trips. "My favorite subject is math." It wasn't a statement so much as a lesson. He was teaching me phrases, correcting my pronunciations and grammar. I repeated whatever he said.

It was only about a mile to the market. We had just started walking and were still close to Javier's father's house. The houses in this area were bigger, nicer than in other parts of town. I was wearing slacks and a top, a kerchief on my head tied at the back. It was hot out already and I noticed a bead of perspiration on Javier's upper lip. "Don't run so much," I said. "You're going to wear yourself out." He laughed, ran back, and took my hand again. I glanced up to a hill nearby. It sounded like a little rock slide had come down the hill. Javier's hand was suddenly slack in my hand and I glanced back in front of us.

"*Eyyyy, puta,*" the first man said. "*Quanto custou?*" Three men stood before us.

"How much does it cost?" Is that what he asked me? Were they asking directions to the mercantile? Javier's hand stiffened in my grip.

"*Bonita,*" said another, and motioned at the ground. They were all young, thickly built, maybe late teens or early twenties. They had dark circles under their eyes like they had been out all night drinking and were just now returning from the clubs. They were motioning us up the hill. "Just keep on walking," Javier said to me, but the three young men were close to us now, gripping us, pushing. A man had me by the elbow and I jerked free and turned to go. "*Onde posso troca dinheiro,*" he said. "Where can I change money?" I took the continued money-talk as a sign they were after my wallet. I had some jewelry on me, not much, a cross around my neck, my college ring. I started talking, blabbering loudly, saying anything I could think of, trying to stall, trying to figure out a next move. They were pushing us again. Shoving. Almost carrying us along. More trees were around us now. It was quieter up the hill, more secluded.

"*Muito caro!*" said the first again. "Very expensive." He grabbed my necklace and pulled it off.

I was through talking. I screamed. A little shock, a little tug was all Javier needed. He wrenched free from the man who held him and took off running. The man yelled and sprinted after him. The other two turned to me. All was a blur from then on. First there was screaming. I remember thrashing violently, struggling to get away. Then one of them hit me in the head with a rock. That was the last thing I remember.

When I awoke some time later, I was in the hospital. My eyes were both blackened. My face and body were cut and deeply bruised. I had been attacked with a machete. At first the doctors thought I had a broken jaw, but they didn't have the right X-ray equipment to check for sure, and it proved to be swollen badly. I underwent a D&C in the hospital to make sure there was no pregnancy.

Javier's running saved my life; I am certain of that. Dashing to get help, he paid the ultimate sacrifice. Later word spread instantly that the American woman was being attacked. People had come running and caught the men in the act. Some Brazilian police officers had arrived just after the first adults and had fought the three men. The officers had overpowered them, the reports said, and then continued beating them before hauling them to jail. The men were charged with robbery, rape, and attempted murder. They'd had guns, so I guess I was lucky in that I lived. In time, and because I didn't die from my wounds, the men were sentenced to life in prison. Brazilian laws leave little room for appeals, so I assume they are still behind bars. I didn't have to testify at their trials, fortunately. In the condition I was in, I wasn't sure if I could have managed.

The doctor I was staying with took care of me in the hospital. I was on a lot of painkillers and sedatives, but through the daze I can still remember his kind face, his sharp eyebrows and bushy mustache. "Miss Suzana," he said gently, "there was much damage. Just so much . . ." Here his voice broke, professional though he was. "As difficult as it is to hear this, Miss Suzana, I must tell you: you may never be able to have children."

It took a week for word of the assault to reach Donna. She rushed to me as soon as she heard. I didn't want any other family with me then, just Donna. I wasn't quite sure why. She came to me as I lay in the hospital bed and we cried together. We sobbed. We sobbed like the women in Bethlehem whose innocent children had just been slaughtered.

After that, great sections of silence filled each day. Donna simply sat with me as I tried to heal. I was in the hospital for some time. The Quixadá police did their reports. Some officials from Fortaleza came and went—I don't remember why. Some of the big guns from the Peace Corps flew down from Washington, D.C. The incident hit the newspapers in the States. Later, because of what had happened to me, the Peace Corps changed their policy: no female volunteer could ever be stationed alone again. I felt a small shred of satisfaction in that, though I'm not positive even that would have helped. I wasn't alone when I was attacked. It was broad daylight. Javier and I were walking in a well-traversed area.

At times in the hospital, I thought about Doug. What would he think of me now? My idea of sex was to get married first and have a beautiful honeymoon. And then beautiful children. The whole beautiful dream was stolen from me. Who would want damaged goods? At least, that's how I felt about myself.

At times, I thought about my father. Now I understood why he hadn't want me to go to Vietnam. I was in and out of consciousness because of the painkillers, but when I was coherent there was a different feeling about everything, about myself, about the world. Everything wasn't wonderful in the world anymore. "Watch out for those cowboys," my father had said so many times. I had met those cowboys now; they were real and they were bastards.

Often, I thought of my mother. I knew she would love me no matter what, but I couldn't face her just yet, although she was who I wanted to see most of all. There on that hill just before I was hit in the head with a rock, I do remember praying to God that I'd see my mother again. I remember that prayer clearly.

Maybe I didn't want to come home to face everybody's questions. Maybe that's still the tension I feel in writing about this even now, so many years later. So much time has passed; so much has healed. But maybe my fear of those questions is what causes me to run upstairs by myself in my Rhode Island house; there, I'm alone and no one can hear me talking this out. No one can hear my true thoughts. I really don't want anyone to hear me, not even my husband, George, and he knows almost everything about me.

I'll say this: I went to Brazil with the Peace Corps to help other people. I truly believe some of them were helped. I fulfilled another chapter of my life's purpose, and I came out stronger and wiser in time.

CHAPTER 6

Undefeated

O NE NIGHT IN IRAQ, I sensed a familiar darkness. I remembered it well because I could recognize its presence in my own life. That night I was called to the hospital where the marines had brought in the body of a 19-year-old soldier. He had the bulky muscles of someone who had been put through his paces in the military for some time now, doing push-ups and sit-ups and squat thrusts and endless running. But he wasn't filled out yet as a grown man is; he was still lean like a boy. He could have been anybody's son; he may have been a red-haired, freckle-faced kid from Milwaukee, or he might have sported a short Irish brush cut like some boy from Providence, or maybe he'd been a cool, sandy-haired California surfer before he joined the army. It was impossible anymore to tell. The young man's girlfriend had broken up with him, and he had put a clip in his rifle and shot himself while standing in a phone booth on base. His uniform was soaked with blood, and a puckered hole had been blown through the center of his skull. I wondered what might have happened if someone had been able to reach him in time, to talk with him, to say something comforting, maybe just to have been there with him when he was in need—maybe he wouldn't have committed suicide.

In a way, I know what it's like to stand in a phone booth with a rifle to my head. That is, I've been to an equivalent place. I have felt this same sort of pull, this temptation to end my life. When I mulled the assault in Quixadá, I wondered what I'd done wrong, as rape victims are prone to do. I wondered if I could have done something differently. Maybe I shouldn't have fought back. Or maybe it was good that I had; maybe that saved my life. The pressure of replaying the horrible incident in my mind gnawed at me. Mornings, I woke up and a constant darkness clouded my mind. The darkness wouldn't leave. It simply wouldn't leave.

One morning, the darkness stood next to me. Still in the hospital in Quixadá, I put my legs over the side of the bed, hoisted myself up, and walked to the bathroom to look in the mirror. Donna helped me. She didn't want me to look at myself yet, but I insisted. I saw the darkness in the mirror: bruises, black eyes, hollow cheeks. Whose face was staring back at me? This wasn't the Sue Corry I knew. I wanted my face back. I wanted my peace of mind again. I was hopeful that the first would return, but I was worried that the latter never would.

A few days later, a plane ticket to Rio de Janeiro was placed in my hand. The Peace Corps was sending me there for ten weeks to recuperate. Donna would go with me. It felt good to have her by my side. If it weren't for Donna, I would have gone back to the States immediately, but she understood what I had been through, so she was who I needed just then. Donna's mission in Brazil had been different from mine. Hers was more flexible, and she could be released from her town more easily. Sending us somewhere to recuperate was sensitive of the Peace Corps officials. If I didn't go somewhere to heal, I'm sure I would have fallen apart soon. Donna and I made the long bus trip from Quixadá to Fortaleza in preparation for our flight to Rio.

While stopped in Fortaleza, I went to the Peace Corps office and telephoned my parents. It was the first time I had talked to them after the assault. It was my decision to hold things in. I was an adult. They knew I had been attacked but didn't know the severity; if they had known, I'm sure my mother would have flown out right then to get me. There was lots of crying on the phone, from my mother as well as from me.

"Come back home, Susan, please," my mother pleaded.

"I'm okay," I said. "I'm okay. I'm okay."

Surely that was a lie, but I wasn't going to leave Brazil just yet. I wasn't from a family of quitters. That's what I had convinced myself of anyway. I truly did want to go back and finish my Peace Corps mission. If I didn't finish what I had started, then it would have undercut any work I had already done there, and if that foundation was blown out from under me, well, then that would have made the assault even harder to bear. To go home at that point would have meant that nothing I did in Brazil had mattered. You see the same sort of reasoning today in Iraq. Some wounded soldiers are given the option of being flown home to the States. A number of these soldiers choose instead to recuperate overseas and rejoin the battle. I know why they make that decision.

My sister was getting married that June. She invited me to be her maid of honor, but I couldn't face everybody yet, not at a wedding. The wedding pictures wouldn't show my black eyes by then, but it was too early to be around that much attention—at least that's what I suspected. The pictures wouldn't show the dark wound in my heart, but it would be there, and it would especially hurt at a wedding, something I felt was forever out of reach for me now. As I was talking to my mother on the phone in Fortaleza, my mind drifted to a news story I had heard years earlier. A girl had been dragged out of a Rhode Island hospital and raped. It was one of those random acts of brutality you hear about from time to time. The girl killed herself soon after. That was the fear I tried to push from my mind. Some people put rifles to their heads in phone booths. Others lose their purpose and sink under the constant waves of emotional pain. They commit suicide, too, but they do it slowly, sometimes over a lifetime. I sensed I would fight that battle for a long while. And that's part of why I chose to stay in Brazil. I wanted to take one conscious step in the direction of not being defeated.

In Rio, Donna and I stayed in the home of a prominent surgeon and his wife. I don't remember if they had kids. They had a big house, money, maids, cars. I think the surgeon was an American doctor working for the government. He spoke fluent English. I don't remember much else. There were still so many clouds in my mind during that time.

When we got there, I didn't do much of anything. I lay on a couch and took walks in the garden and waited for the swelling to go down. Checkups at the hospital were part of my routine, but eventually there were fewer of them. I just needed to be somewhere quiet where my body could do its own restorative work. The doctor's house was right by the water. Donna and I looked out the windows and saw the ocean. Within a few weeks, I started getting up more, and we got out and around and into the city. Rio was so different from Quixadá. It was a swirl of images: the Copacabana Beach, the song about the girl from Ipanema, stores filled with perfume and sequins and ball gowns, sidewalks filled with women wearing beautiful shoes, men with expensive suits and watches. I had just come from an area where most of the population struggled to afford the most basic of shoes, a region where kids often didn't have two solid meals per day. The doctor and his wife took us to a party at the American embassy.

I tried black caviar for the first time, but it tasted like licking a salt shaker. Later, we watched the parade for carnival with its huge floats of sculpted lions and gigantic peacocks, candles by the thousands, dancers, twirlers, acrobats, jugglers, cymbal crashers, horn blowers, and rows and rows of cheering people hanging out of office building windows.

Despite the culture shock I felt at seeing the lavishness of Rio, I wasn't mad at the Brazilian people for what had happened to me in their country. I struggled to put the culture shock in perspective, even to savor the moments Donna and I had away from dirt and flies and lines of sick people standing for hours in the sun. People are people. Rich people. Poor people. We're all in this together. It's like being in Iraq: individual Iraqis are never the enemy; the terrorist organizations are.

Maybe it was in everybody's best interest to have me out of town for a while until news of the assault died down. After several weeks in Rio, I chose to go back to Quixadá. I wasn't scared. Donna was stationed with me this time. The town—with its 1880s storefronts and dirt roads, its donkeys and chickens, its women in dresses and men in slacks—was the same. Donna and I stepped off the bus after the 12-hour ride from Fortaleza, and things felt okay. There was more work to be done.

We rented a little villa of our own. Most Peace Corps volunteers do this. Initially, I had been stationed with the doctor and his family so that I could learn the language better. Donna and I could have stayed with him again, but his house was farther from the center of town. Maybe I was scared to go back to a location where every day I'd need to pass the area where I was assaulted. The place Donna and I rented was next to the hospital. We could walk across the street and be at work in a minute.

It felt different to be renting a room with Donna. It felt good.

It was like we were in college again except that there was no pressure to study every night. Without consciously talking about it, I believe, we both made decisions to keep living as normally as possible. It was our strategy to combat the lingering effects of the assault. And why not? Apart from the black caviar, I had enjoyed my taste of Rio. Now here we were, two single women living unencumbered in a foreign country. We were young and determined and going forward.

Every Saturday night, little concerts were held all over Quixadá. They weren't concerts in the sense of being huge theater shows. Mostly they were held at club venues where friendly locals gathered to laugh and dance and eat barbecued pork and hoist beers. One band, I don't even remember its name now, was comprised of five musicians: a wild-man drummer who flailed about at the back of the stage; a sullen bassist who stood stock-still and wore dark sunglasses even at night; a Buddy Holly–styled guitarist who jitterbugged in his pressed slacks, button-down shirt, and nerdy glasses; and two smiling singers who grabbed the mics up front. They were mostly a cover band who belted out early 1970s American top 40 hits: "Bad, Bad Leroy Brown" by Jim Croce, "Free Bird" by Lynyrd Skynard, "Let's Get It On" by Marvin Gaye—songs like that, all strummed with passion and verve and huge grins. The band packed in the crowds every Saturday night. Francey and Marcello, the two frontmen on stage, looked so free with the lights and electricity and the sweat that ran down their foreheads by the night's end. The band's guitarist was frequently off-key, and the bass player looked like he was just learning, and I doubted the band would ever make it big as musicians, but I'm not sure they even wanted that. To them, it was all about being young and in a band and singing American pop songs as loudly as they could.

"Sue, they're asking us if we want to go to the lake with them next Saturday afternoon," Donna said. She was smiling, but her forehead showed tiny worry lines. She had just bought us two Cokes from the bar. "Francey and Marcello—the guys from the band. They want us to go with them. At least that's what I think they said. Neither one of them speak very good English."

"What did you tell them?"

"I said sure."

I gulped. I figured that after the assault I'd never want to see another guy again. But here I was being asked out on a date. Francey and Marcello were offstage now. The cool rock-and-roll gods of Quixadá had both grabbed beers from somewhere and had sauntered over to us.

"Boa noite!" Francey said to me. *"Oi, tudo bem?"*

Just casual greetings from boys to girls. Francey was shorter, with hairy forearms and a thick neck. Marcello was taller, with big eyes and a strong Portuguese nose.

"Come on, pretty girl, let's dance," Francey said in his best English.

He took me by the hand and we went out on the club's dance floor. The opening guitar riff to "Long Cool Woman in a Black Dress" by the Hollies had started to blast from a turntable somewhere. Donna and Marcello were following us. Donna gave me a little grin.

"It's okay," she yelled to me. "It really is okay."

And then we were dancing. All of us. Just swirling in a mass of dancing young people, dancing in a friendly little club in Quixadá, and as we danced people clapped Francey and Marcello on the back and said things like "Great show man!" and "Your music is so fabulous." The boys from the band were all out on the floor now, the wild-man drummer throwing around his arms and legs all by himself, the cool bass player cheek to cheek with a Brazilian girl feigning a slow dance like the Fonz at Arnold's Drive-In, the Buddy Holly guitarist throwing back his head and laughing. Soon we were all laughing, laughing at something or other, and we were all dancing, dancing, and I shook my shoulders a little bit and for once I imagined myself having fun. And then it was fun. It was really fun. I was actually having fun again.

We went to the lake on Saturday afternoon, Francey and Marcello and Donna and me, then to the marketplace to buy things to make for dinner before their show. That night we returned to the same club where Francey and Marcello sang. They howled on stage and turned their amps' volume controls up past 11, and we all danced in front of the stage with our arms above our heads. We had a barbecue the next afternoon and a lot of their friends came over, boys and girls, and we cooked and ate and laughed and told jokes. Nothing was too wild, no one was drunk or obnoxious; it was just fun, the kind of fun most kids had when they were in college, except Donna and I had been too preoccupied with our nurses' training then.

Francey kissed me goodnight after a week of dating, and I let him. I didn't turn away when he kissed me, and I liked that I didn't turn away. It didn't feel like fireworks, not like I had felt when I imagined Doug kissing me. But Francey's kiss just felt sweet, and I liked that it felt sweet. I had never had a real boyfriend. I guess Francey was my first. I felt normal. We went out more after that. We went to the lake, to the market, to the concerts, to other people's houses for dinner. Doug still wrote me from time to time, and I wrote him back. I think my crush for Doug never diminished, but he was too far away and probably not interested in me anyway. And I didn't think he would ever be if I told him what I had been through. But Francey was right next to me in Quixadá. He wanted to hold my hand, and he wanted to look in my eyes as he sang from the stage, and everybody in town knew Francey with his hairy forearms and thick neck, and there was a lot of protection in being the girlfriend of a local man whom everybody knew.

Our medical work began again, too. The miniposts were really taking off, and we continued training local girls to run them and to work at the hospital. We started up our English-language tutoring again, our vaccine campaigns, our application of curatives, our child care lessons. It felt like things were really coming together—we were cooperating with several local agencies and working jointly to bring better health care to the area. My mother, a teacher who knew what kids liked, sent me goody bags from home filled with treats like chocolates and cookies as well as toys like yo-yos and jacks to pass out. She also sent whole bunches of stuff: clothes for little kids, socks, T-shirts. That was one way I think she felt like she could support our continued efforts in Quixadá.

I loved the hands-on health care we were providing. I loved working with the mothers and children from poorer villages. I especially loved the babies. In Brazilian hospitals, doctors rarely deliver babies. Nurses do—that is, when babies are even delivered at hospitals. In the outlying areas, women usually just squat and get the job done. There's often a midwife to help. Sometimes it's a nurse, but usually it's just an older woman in the village who's been delivering babies for a while.

The doctor with whom I had stayed became more involved with administrative duties in the hospital, so I began to spend more time working in the miniposts with Helena, another Brazilian doctor from the hospital. She was a few years older than I was, single, with reddish hair and a good grasp of English. We still went out with whole teams of people: a driver, several nurses' aides, the teeth-pulling dentist, and Donna and me. Helena struck a good balance between seriousness and fun. She knew how to roll up her sleeves and work, and she believed that people learned best by doing things for themselves. We were out at a minipost one weekend when a small boy tapped us on the shoulder and said his mother was ready to give birth. Would we come help? We assured him we'd be there in a hurry.

"Okay," Helena said when we arrived at the shack, "it's your turn on this one, Suzana."

"Me? I can't deliver a baby. I'm still new at this."

"That's how you'll learn, then."

The woman was lying on a small pallet. A few other kids were milling about. This would be her fifth baby. *"Obrigada,"* the mother said. "Thank you." She was panting, her face in a grimace. The contractions were close. It wouldn't be long.

We shooed the children outside as politely as we could, then helped the mother be as comfortable as possible. We tried to make the area hygienic. When she was dilated to nine centimeters, the baby's head appeared and I helped support it while she slowed her pushing. During the delivery I talked nonstop, as I do whenever I'm nervous, but I remember thinking that firemen deliver babies while trapped in burning buildings, so if they could there, then I could here. One shoulder was out, then the other, then the baby slid out all at once. It was a girl. She was gooey and warm and a good color, the most beautiful thing I had ever seen. I cleaned her mouth and nose, and she gave loud cries to announce her arrival to the world. I cut the cord and sutured the woman's tear. It was an easy delivery. I was glad.

"Obrigada, obrigada," the mother kept whispering. I wasn't sure why she was so grateful. She had given birth before, probably alone. Maybe that's why she was so grateful this time.

Helena gave me a grin. "Not too bad, Suzana," she said, then turned to the mother. "You have a beautiful little girl there. Have you thought about what you're going to name her?"

The mother turned to me and asked me a question. In all the excitement, we hadn't gotten past anything other than the basic communications of the delivery. The woman smiled and looked at her baby, now nursing on her breast. "Her name is Suzana," the mother said in Portuguese. "Suzana, in your honor."

Baby Suzana. She was my namesake, born here in a tiny town on the other side of the world. I held the baby and touched her face, her tiny hands; I stroked her soft hair. She was crying still, her breaths coming softly in healthy yelps, and I knew deep down that it was okay for me to have returned to Quixadá. Moments like this were why I came to do this mission.

My mother sent a flood of things for baby Suzana and her mother: little outfits, toys, and clothes for the other children in the family. Anytime we went back to that post, I loaded up whatever my mother had sent and gave them to the family privately. It felt good to have this family connection with the baby named after me.

In August, I went home to Rhode Island for a ten-day visit. It was eight months after the attack, and my face and body had both healed by then. My sister and I sat side by side on a couch and pored over her wedding photos together, and I understood that she understood why I had needed to miss her wedding. My sister and I might have looked different on the outside, but in many ways we were cut from the same cloth. We cared about the same issues: family, love, support, giving people space when needed. It felt good to be home. I had missed my mother and father so much. My mother cooked for me—meatloaf, chicken potpie, rotisserie lamb with crusted mustard. She made my favorite dessert, her wonderful brownie pudding—chocolate and rich. I ate and ate and ate.

When the trip to Rhode Island was over, I flew back to Quixadá. There was still another year to go. Being at home was wonderful, but I was more determined than ever to finish what I started. I wasn't going to be defeated.

THE SECOND YEAR in the Peace Corps passed quickly. Near the end of my service in Quixadá, I became project supervisor. The work was in full progress and being carried on by the girls we had trained. On December 6, 1974, my service officially ended. All the remaining Americans who had started with the original group and were able to attend gathered in Fortaleza for a big going-away celebration. Doug was there. He was still tall and tanned and smiling, and happy as ever to see me. We gave our home addresses to each other and promised to write. Donna chose to extend her stay in Quixadá for a few more months. Things between her and Marcello had heated up, and she wondered if maybe he was the one. I didn't feel that way about Francey. He was my first boyfriend and a great guy, but I knew our relationship wasn't going to amount to anything more. I didn't want it to. Francey and I weren't meant to be together forever. I planned to get my master's degree in public health back in the States and continue my career in nursing. My mission was to keep moving.

Boston University awarded me a full graduate scholarship, but the program didn't begin until September 1975. So I took a job for several months at Rhode Island Hospital doing regular medical/surgical nursing. I hated it. It was just all this technical stuff. We were kept too busy to be able to talk to patients, to really get to know them. This kind of nursing was not for me.

The start of graduate school seemed a long way off, too long maybe, and for another moment I toyed with the idea that maybe nursing wasn't going to be my life's work.

I didn't like the way people looked at me in the States either. Or maybe it was the way I thought they looked at me. The 70s were in full swing when I returned, and everybody seemed to be into disco, David Cassidy, and long floral granny dresses. America had moved on without me. It had become fast all of a sudden and too cynical. Maybe there was something wrong with me. Maybe I would never fit in. Or maybe people could see what had been done to me—that was my greatest fear. I consoled myself by eating. The more I ate, the more I disappeared. I became invisible to prying eyes, the eyes of men on the street. Francey was back home in Brazil, Doug was gone, and my team of friends and coworkers was elsewhere: I felt all alone in a country I didn't understand anymore. I wanted to go back to Brazil, to a place I understood, to a place where I could feel normal again. However, I no longer knew what normal felt like.

So I ate. Graduate school began and I raced through the program, and I ate. If I hurried, I could complete the program in one year. That put more pressure on things, so I ate. I lived at home and commuted to school each way on the bus. My mother typed my papers for me. Somewhere in there, I climbed on a bathroom scale, white towel clutched around my middle, and looked down. The scale read 219 pounds.

I wanted to stop overeating, but I didn't know how. I was committing that slow type of suicide that I had worried about earlier. I was caught in a continual cycle of feeling hopeless and turning to an old habit to feel better, but that old habit was destroying me. I didn't know whom to talk to or where to turn. I tried diets, with no success. Finally, I paid $500 to a dentist and had my jaw wired shut. It was a desperate move. The idea was that I could ingest only liquids, and a liquid diet would take the pounds off.

When I came home from having the procedure done, my mother took one look at me and said, "Susan, we love you, and we want you to lose weight. But this is not the way to lose it."

I didn't say anything. I couldn't. It was hard to speak with my jaw wired shut. Mom marched me back to the dentist the next day and had my jaw unwired. Then she took me to Weight Watchers. That was a better solution.

Two other things helped as well. I found a nursing instructor in the community health program at Boston University who became my mentor. She did what I wanted to do—she helped people. Her life's work was that simple. My graduate thesis provided an overview of community services for elderly people in Rhode Island. As part of the thesis, I wrote a pamphlet in Spanish, English, and Portuguese. I wrote it at the last minute and received an A.

And then I decided to go back to Brazil.

When I was with the Peace Corps, I had toured the ship known as SS *HOPE* when it was docked in Brazil. It was an old World War II destroyer that had been converted into a traveling medical center by the organization Project HOPE (Health Opportunities for People Everywhere). Staffed with doctors and nurses, SS *HOPE* motored to various ports around the world to provide health care for the poor. Late in 1974, the ship itself was mothballed, but the project continued in stationary facilities. As soon as I got my master's degree, I was on my way. I had already done my interview with Project HOPE in Washington, D.C., and they placed me in the city of Natal, the capital of Rio Grande do Norte, a state in northeastern Brazil. Natal was a big city, maybe 600,000 people then, with white sandy beaches and skyscrapers and amazing sunsets over the nearby Potengi River.

I went alone this time, but I had no reservations about going back alone to Brazil. I just wanted to be in a place I knew. It felt comfortable. This was what I wanted to do, help people, particularly poor people. I didn't think of hooking up with Francey again. He was a few hours away from where I was stationed, but it was over between us. There was no nasty breakup or anything; the relationship had just run its course.

Working for Project HOPE instead of volunteering for the Peace Corps meant that I made more than 11 cents per hour, but nothing close to what I would have made in the States. I didn't mind. I was motivated by service, adventure, the thought of feeling normal again. The clinic where I worked was right on the water. I met a lot of nice nurses, doctors and dentists, a whole group of new friends. I rented a room in Natal with another nurse who worked with Project HOPE. We could see the water from our villa. She had gone to UCLA and was very smart. As soon as I arrived, I began to diet even more than I had at home. I never felt prouder than the day my bathroom scale read 120 pounds. I was back. The real me was back.

Natal wasn't entirely safe, but I didn't feel frightened. I felt older by then, wiser. One of the Project HOPE dentists didn't listen to advice and rented a beach house farther out of town. He threw parties for all the team members, and I met him several times. One day at the hospital, a team member rushed in, his face ashen, and announced that the dentist had been robbed and murdered. It was a senseless tragedy. From then on, I felt increasingly wary about the city. I never went anywhere alone if I could help it. I realized it's a dangerous world everywhere; still, I was beginning again to feel mostly safe and the optimism of youth was returning to me.

My work with Project HOPE was similar to what I did in Quixadá, except this time we were based in a large city. Each day we loaded up jeeps and traveled into the interior region and set up small health clinics to provide medical services for poor people living on the outskirts. We also spent a lot of time working in the hospital in Natal. We were not observers this time; rather, we were the experienced ones with graduate degrees—adults, grown-ups. I taught classes in nursing, health, and hygiene.

Beto was one of my students. I'm not sure what Beto was doing in my class, come to think about it—he was studying to become a plastic surgeon. What would a surgical student have been doing in a nursing class? Maybe he just sat in on one so that he could take a good look at me. His real name was Herbert—how they got Beto out of that, I don't know. He was serious and studious, tall, quiet, handsome, with a nice smile. He spoke seven languages fluently and had gone to high school in America. Beto's father was English, his mother Brazilian. His family owned one of the largest soft drink manufacturing operations in the country. His sister was a doctor at the hospital, his brother an engineering student. They were a family with wealth and privilege, ambition and success. Beto invited all the Americans from Project HOPE over to his family's home for parties. They lived in a beautiful house with fountains and elegant rooms with high ceilings. A flurry of butlers, cooks, and maids was constantly about.

Beto liked me. He pursued me. I said yes. We were serious quickly. This relationship felt way different from the one I'd had with Francey, which had been based solely on fun. It felt different from my friendship with Doug, someone always out of reach. Beto was here and now and amazing, and he wanted me, and he wanted something long-term, and he was someone I could see myself actually settling down with. He loved to go out for dinner. He loved to go for walks. He loved to buy me fancy dresses, typical Brazilian dresses, very colorful and elegant. They offered a taste of what Beto as a husband could provide. Shortly after Christmas, Beto flew with me to Rhode Island to meet my parents. They absolutely loved him. He was polite, intelligent, everything a family could want for their daughter. He immediately fell in love with little Katie, my sister's first baby, and she with him. *Beto would make a great father,* I thought, *if only I could have children.* But that wasn't talked about, not then. We were having too much fun. While in Rhode Island, we took a side trip up to Niagara Falls, just the two of us. We were stranded by a snowstorm on the way back and we holed up in a romantic hideaway.

The only thing that didn't feel right about this period of my life was my chest. I had always felt top-heavy. It was a medical issue for me as much as a self-consciousness thing. My bra straps used to cut into me until my shoulders bled. So back in Brazil I opted for breast reduction surgery. Beto's sister's husband, also a surgeon, performed the operation for me for free. I went from a DD to a C cup. It was the best thing for my health I ever did.

Beto didn't seem to mind. He gave me a ring shortly afterward. Maybe it was an engagement ring in his mind, but I thought of it more as a promise ring. "Would you ever think of settling down with me in Brazil?" Beto asked. He asked it more than once. The offer was definitely there: marriage to a family-oriented young surgeon with a wealthy background. What more could a woman ever want? This could really be it. He was constantly on my mind. Should I? Or shouldn't I? That was the continual question bashing itself through my mind. I knew getting married to Beto would mean moving to Brazil for good, and I wasn't sure I wanted that. I knew it would also mean giving up my career for good. His culture expected that from married women. So I didn't know what to do.

No, that's not true. I did know what to do. I really did know.

When my commitment with Project HOPE was up, I flew back to the States. Still, Beto's offer was there. We kept in contact through letters. I flew back once to see him. I continued to wear my promise ring.

When I imagined a life married to Beto, I envisioned cocktail parties and ball gowns and credit cards and afternoon tea brought to me by a maid. Beto and I could adopt, maybe, and I could see Beto bending down over our baby's crib. He would be wearing a suit and his hands would be clean. He would have just come home from the hospital. And I would have just returned from the mall.

Beto was as perfect as I could imagine a man just then, but it wasn't the perfect relationship. I was never going to be the kind of wife he was looking for. I was too independent. I had things I still wanted to do, things that mattered to me. Maybe they would matter—really matter—to other people who would need the medical services I had learned how to offer by then. I had come through this part of my life undefeated for a reason. In time, I stopped wearing his ring. Beto and I gradually drifted apart, forever.

CHAPTER 7

From a Small, Dark Office

WHEN I ARRIVED back in the States after my tour with Project HOPE, it was 1978 and I was 28 years old. I didn't have a husband, and I already knew, deep down, that I could not marry Beto. I didn't have a job or any good leads. I didn't have a child of my own or even any hope of ever having one. I had no specific idea of what to do next. All I had was that continuing ache within me to do something that mattered.

By now I knew that nursing was going to be my life, but I didn't want to start working in a stateside hospital again. Doing so had always made me feel stuck. I wondered what else a nurse could do. One of my first ideas was to apply for a position with the World Health Organization (WHO), the United Nations public health arm. I was soon offered a big job with WHO, but I delayed the acceptance. Something didn't seem quite right about the position for me. My mother sensed my churning.

"Sue, what about being a school nurse?" she asked. She poured me another glass of orange juice, passed me the butter to put on my pancakes, then sat at the breakfast table to join me. Though it was still early morning, August heat waves rose outside our window. "It's not as glamorous as the United Nations, but you get summers off." She gave a little grin.

"Oh, I don't know, Mom. I know you always loved teaching, but—"

"But what? Not enough adventure for a world traveler like you?"

I smiled. "That's not what I meant."

Mom tilted her head slightly and raised her chin. "Kids need what people like you have to offer, Sue. Seriously. Some of these schools today, they're tough places. They're real war zones."

My ears perked up at that last phrase. I had attended private Catholic schools and thus knew little about public schools in Rhode Island, so I figured I'd investigate the option my mother was proposing. Maybe I could work for a year or two at a public school and see how I liked it. I doubted I'd stay long. Some other adventure must be right around the corner.

Three inner-city Providence high schools were hiring that fall: Central, Mount Pleasant, and Hope. Central High intrigued me the most. It came with a horrible reputation: the worst of the worst. People were still talking about the big race riot that had been waged the year before, during which kids went running through the school swinging baseball bats at each other. The blacks and the Italians were big rivals at the time. The news reports consistently talked about gang activity, shootings, drug arrests, and mob fights at Central. The school building itself was old and shabby, built in 1927. It was the largest high school in Providence, with about 2,200 teenagers packed into the joint. People considered it a place of constant tension, outright violence, and little hope. "Why would you ever want to work at Central?" a nurse friend of mine asked when I told her I'd applied. "You want to get yourself killed?"

I interviewed at Central with Principal Arthur Zarrella. He gave me a fatherly smile from behind his desk. "So what makes you want to be a school nurse, Miss Corry, particularly at Central?

It involves a lot more than giving out Band-Aids, you know. And, if you came on board here, I'd *want* you to make it a lot more than that. We're starting to make some real changes around here. That's the type of team player I'm looking for."

"I come from a long line of teachers," I said. "My mother was a teacher. My grandmother was a teacher. My sister is a teacher. We've got it in our blood."

"It comes down to caring for the students we've got here today. Most of them in this school don't come from families where they have much opportunity. That's our job, Miss Corry. To care about them so that they can see their true potential. It's no small order, and it's not for anybody who's easily intimidated. Is that a task you think you're up for?"

I liked Principal Zarrella immediately. He was a quiet man on the exterior, married with four kids, yet I gauged him as not the type who was easily ruffled. He was fairly new to the school and had some good plans to breathe life into its halls. I might not have had all the educator lingo down yet, but I could tell he saw potential in me and, more important, that he cared a great deal for the kids and staff under his care. He liked that I had my master's degree already and that I could speak Spanish and Portuguese fluently. I would need to get my teaching certificate and become a full-fledged teacher in addition to being a nurse, but I could take university classes concurrently with the job. There were other people applying, but Principal Zarrella hired me on the spot.

School began that September. On my first day I was ushered back to the nurse's office. It was small, dark, and dreary. There was a desk and an old metal filing cabinet. Not much else. My job was to make sure all the students stayed healthy so that they could learn. I wasn't sure of everything that would involve, but I figured I'd find out soon enough.

Standing in the door to my office, I watched a never-ending stream of students rush to their first class. Nearly all the kids, both boys and girls, were dressed in T-shirts and faded blue jeans. Central had a loose dress code in place. Students could wear most anything they liked as long as they didn't display gang colors. Bandannas were strictly against rules. Long hair sprouted everywhere. A few girls wore tube tops. Dark jackets seemed to be hip, even though the weather was still warm. The final bell rang and the halls emptied. All was quiet.

I was just about to head back into my office when I heard a door close. A girl exited the bathroom and sauntered down the hall toward me. Her eyes were caked with dark eye shadow. She was chewing gum and smacked it loudly as she came near. She wasn't hurrying. She wasn't even carrying a book. Our eyes locked. Her nose wrinkled and she shot an icy death stare in my direction.

"I'm pretty sure that bell means you're supposed to be in class already," I said. I was instantly a teacher.

"What do you care?"

"Well, I care that you get an education. And I hope you care, too. In case you've forgotten, that's why you're in school. What class are you supposed to be in right now?"

"Math." The girl blew an enormous bubble and popped it.

"My strong suggestion is that you head there right away."

She stopped chewing. She was young, maybe 14, with dark hair parted in the middle and a few freckles scattered across her Roman nose. Boys would have thought she was cute in a tough-girl sort of way.

"Who are you anyway? How come I ain't never seen you around here?" she asked.

"My name's Miss Corry. I'm the new school nurse."

"School nurse, huh? Well, I got a headache. Real bad. That's why I can't go to math class today. My head's bustin' wide open. Honest."

There was something in the way she said "honest" that made me want to believe her. She sounded like she was used to not being believed. I decided to give her the benefit of the doubt. "Okay, come on into my office. I'll get you a Tylenol."

The girl looked surprised at the invitation and entered the nurse's office with me.

"What's your name?" I asked.

Her tone shifted to snarly again. "Angie. Like an angel. Except I'm a bad angel. You Catholic?"

"Yeah, why do you ask?"

"None of your business. Can I sit down? My head's killing me."

I fumbled to find a Tylenol and a consent form so she could take the medicine.

"You got lossa kids?" Angie asked. She sat.

"No, I'm not married."

"What would you name your kids if you had any?"

"Oh, I don't know." I watched her out of the corners of my eyes as I fumbled through desk drawers. I remembered I had some Tylenol in my purse. "For a boy, I've always liked the name Doug. I don't know what I'd name a girl. Maybe Margaret, after my mother. How about you?"

"I'd name it something." Her voice sounded too quick, like she was closing that part of the conversation. She pointed at the brown bag under my desk. "Hey, is that your lunch? Did you bring lunch today? Can I have half of your sandwich?"

I found the Tylenol bottle and gave her a pill. "Are you hungry already, Angie? It was just breakfast an hour ago."

She sprang up. "Forget I asked. I don't want your old sandwich anyway. I got to go." She headed for the door.

"Hey, wait a minute. Relax." I decided to forgo any definitive conclusions on when the girl last ate. "I packed extra today. Turkey breast with mayo. It's really good. My mother made it for me."

Angie shrugged, sat back down, and took half the sandwich. "Your mother packs your lunch?"

I grinned. "Well, why not? My mother's a great cook. Me? I only know how to make toast. Doesn't your mother ever cook for you?"

Angie's eyebrows lowered, her lips thinned. "She'd never cook anything for me." The sandwich half was gone in a jiffy. My silence must have prompted her to continue. "She's not my mother anyway. She's my foster mom." She pointed at my lunch again and gave a little twist with her eyebrows. I handed her the other half of the sandwich. Angie munched it thoughtfully. For a few minutes all was silent.

"How about your dad? Does he cook?"

"He's a goddamn son of a bitch."

Angie's sudden words bounced off the empty walls of the office. I didn't know what to say to something like that. Angie didn't look like she was inviting further questions. She wiped her mouth with the back of her hand. "Well, I gotta go," she said. "Thanks for the lunch."

"Yeah . . . yeah, you should probably get back to class. Here's a note so you can get in."

"I don't know if I can go to math. I still got this headache."

I looked into her eyes as closely as she would let me. "I know you can make it today, Angie. If things get worse, come see me. In fact, come back and see me tomorrow and let me know how you're doing with . . . with that headache. Right now, you've got to get yourself an education."

Angie stuck her tongue out at me. Little bits of sandwich clung to it. I could see she wasn't angry. "You're pretty strict, Miss Corry, you know that?"

"Hey, it's my job, right?"

The corners of Angie's mouth quivered almost as if she wanted to smile, I think. She left.

My job? What really was my job? A school nurse is a mother to some. Angie sounded like she needed a social worker. I was stuck in a small, dark office without any Tylenol. This place was going to need a lot of work. I rolled up my sleeves and took an inventory of what had to get done.

Some months passed. Slowly I grew into my new role as a school nurse. Principal Zarrella was doing a great job in leading the school toward the future. The staff all loved him. Even the kids seemed to respect his presence. But despite the progress, an uneasy tension seemed to continue in the school. It was hard to put your finger on it, exactly, but things felt shaky, like the ground in front of an active volcano that hasn't gone off in a while. Something big could erupt at any time. You know it is going to happen, but you don't know when.

In the meantime, work continued. The little nurse's office was becoming much more than when it started. I conducted health screenings, checking students' vision, hearing, dental hygiene, and overall health. I provided health counseling for students with chronic illnesses, taught nutrition and disease prevention to students and their parents, and made sure state immunization laws were upheld. I earned my teaching certificate in time and taught health education. I became the resource person: I detected, planned, treated, referred, and followed up.

One afternoon just after lunch, the ground shook. Angry shouts blasted down the hall. I briefly put my hands over my ears at first. I remember that precisely because I remember touching the big hoop earrings I had on that day.

"Apologize! You need to apologize!"

"You shut up—shut up! Shut up! Shut up!"

"Get outta here, you trash!"

The first voice was almost screaming. The second was a shouting sneer. Then the voices mixed together, one high, long barrage of yelling and swearing. Then came thuds. Kids' bodies were hitting the lockers.

I was running. Principal Zarrella was running. Assistant Principal Joe DeStefano was running. We were all running. In the middle of the hall was a screaming, yelling, hitting, chewing mob. As best I could see, two kids were beating each other in the middle of it. Girls. They were wailing on each other. A throng of kids ringed the fighters. Side fights were breaking out within the ring. Some kids tried to hold each other back. Others egged each other on.

"You get her, Angie," someone yelled. "You teach that bitch a lesson!"

As I got closer, I could see that the girl who was fighting Angie was bigger and taller. I didn't recognize her. She was flailing away with her fists at Angie's face. Angie lunged at the girl's middle. The girl flew backward into the lockers. That was the thudding sound. The taller girl shoved Angie off and kicked at her knees. Angie toppled and splattered on the floor. The taller girl kicked her in the ribs, then kicked her in the face. Angie rolled over and sprang up, clutching her stomach, blood streaming from a cut under her eye. I could see Principal Zarrella trying to get close. He was just about within arm's reach of the taller girl when four leering senior guys blocked his path, apparently enjoying the show. I shimmied between the outer ring and grabbed

Angie by the sleeve, the other girl by the wrist. Principal Zarrella shook the senior boys off and pivoted to stop another side fight that raged nearby. Out of the corner of my eye, I saw Assistant Principal DeStefano pulling one kid off another in the midst of a different side fight. We were all in the thick of it now, outnumbered if the mob decided to turn against us, quite in danger if we dared to think about our odds.

"Stop it right now!" I shouted. "Break it up—both of you."

The taller girl lunged for Angie this time. When Angie swung back, her sleeve caught one of my hoop earrings and hot liquid flowed down the side of my face. The other girl swung with an open hand. I ducked, Angie moved in, and the blow fell on her shoulder. Angie bent down and screamed at the girl: "Apologize! You need to apologize!"

"Never! I'll never apologize to a whore like you!"

Angie straightened up quick and struck the taller girl alongside the jaw. The taller girl snaked in with a left hook to Angie's head. I was right in the middle.

I don't remember exactly how long it took to break up the fight. Some teachers refused to get involved in fights. If fights happened and they were around to witness the action, they just called the police, sat back, and waited. I didn't blame them for not wanting to enter a fray. Still, it was hard not to get involved when kids were getting hurt. It must have been close to ten minutes before we got this one—and all the side fights it created—under control.

"YOU KNOW, MISS CORRY, I didn't really mean to do that." The halls were cleared, and Angie sat on the cot in my office. I was putting ice under her eye. Another staff member was taking care of the taller girl in a different room. Various kids were waiting outside my office with bloody noses and bleeding lips. The girls' guardians had both been called, as had the guardians of several other kids involved in side fights. The police were on their way to get a report.

"Are you saying you didn't mean to start the fight?" I asked.

"No. That bitch had it coming. I mean, I'm sorry about your ear."

My ear was burning where I had already taped a heavy wad of gauze to it. The earring had pulled out and ripped through my lobe. The earring's back must have gotten snagged on its way through, because a chunk of flesh from the lower part of my ear was completely missing. I was heading over to the ER just as soon as I bandaged up Angie. I was pretty sure I needed stitches. Maybe plastic surgery. I doubted I'd ever be able to wear an earring again in that ear.

"I really didn't mean to," Angie repeated. "Can you forgive me, Miss Corry?"

"I don't know exactly what to say, Angie. You can't go through life angry at everybody, you know?"

Angie squinted, confused. "No, you're wrong. If someone sticks it to you, you need to bash his brains in." Her face froze into a glare. "That's what you sure feel like, anyway."

"That's true, Angie. You sure feel that way. People hurt you, and you want to hurt them back. But fighting is rarely the solution. All it succeeds in doing is getting you more hurt." I held a clean compress to another cut on Angie's face.

"So what is, then?" she asked.

"What's what?"

"The solution?"

I sighed. "I guess it's the answer to that question you just asked me a minute ago."

Susan and her sister Ellen-Ann on a picnic with their parents

Susan making her First Communion, while her sister and brothers look on lovingly

Susan at Sacred Heart Grammar School

Clockwise from top: Susan holding her beloved cat Tiger; her Aunt Ellen; and her mother

Ellen-Ann, Jack, Susan, and Bill having fun on vacation

Front row: Susan, Karen, and Ellen-Ann Back row: Jack, Toni, George, Bill, and Steve on R&R Christmas 2006

Christine, Susan, and Donna
in Brazil with the Peace Corps
in 1972

Susan working with Project Hope
in Natal, Brazil, in 1977
alongside her nursing students

Susan and her students in her office at Central High School

Susan's first date with George at Central High's Christmas Ball

Susan dancing with her father at her wedding on August 25, 1985

Susan taking a break at Ft. Devens, MA with the late Sergeant First Class Joe Forcier and Sergeant First Class Ray Arbrige from the 455th Field Hospital

Lieutenant Colonel Elaine D'Antuono and Susan enjoying the local fare while on a humanitarian mission to Honduras

Susan and Colonel Deniece Barnett-Scott, whom she first met in Guatemala and who later became Susan's own doctor in Iraq

George and Susan in Boston at her going away ceremony prior to leaving for Fort McCoy, WI

Lieutenant Christopher Manion and Susan in Marez, Iraq

The famous public health team of Specialist Tice, Major Adloff, Susan, and Sergeant First Class Cirella, returning via their "limo" from Baghdad's Irish highway—one of the most dangerous routes in Iraq

Susan's own "Band of Sisters"
in Al Asad, Iraq: Captain Michele
Diamond, Susan, Lieutenant
Colonel Gloria Vignone, and
Captain Bertha Maloof

In her office in Al Asad, Susan shows off a picture of
George, Rosie, Shaggy, and their Ritz Carlton Lion while
Major Carliss Townes looks on.

1SG Shirley Martino
teaching Susan to
cook for the troops—
broken arm and all

The Corrys, Higginbothams, Luzes, and the D'Antuonos at the Luz family's "happiest place on Earth"

Susan and George, loving life 25 years later, still together through it all

"What's that?"

"You asked if I would forgive you," I said.

"Oh yeah. So . . . do you?"

I checked the cut to see if Angie's bleeding had stopped. It hadn't. I continued to apply pressure on her cheek.

I nodded.

THERE WERE MORE FIGHTS at Central, lots of them. There were angry parents. Angry administrators. Frustrated teachers. Failing students. There was the boy who showed up in my office on a Monday morning asking if I could change the dressing to his wound. He had been shot over the weekend in a gang fight. Something similar happened nearly every Monday morning, and changing dressings on gunshot wounds got to be routine after a while.

I also took care of a girl who tried to commit suicide in a school bathroom. Strangely enough, her story has a happy ending.

She sliced her wrists open with a razor blade and let her blood spurt over her head until someone discovered her and ran to get me. I had seen incidents of self-cutting before, the horrible attempts at getting attention that sometimes happen in teenage and young-adult circles, but this wasn't cutting. This girl wanted to be gone forever. We bandaged her thickly and sent her by ambulance to the hospital. Later, we found out why she wanted to kill herself: her foster father was sexually abusing her. The goddamn son of a bitch.

The girl lived. We helped her get into a new foster home and hooked her up with counseling services. A few months later, she came back to school, and when she did, she came to work with me. I wanted to keep a close eye on how she was doing. Each day for an hour she came to file records in my office, but we did more talking than actual filing.

Some years later, after her graduation, the girl married a good guy and had beautiful kids of her own. She named them good, strong names. I think she had been thinking about those names for quite a while. She came back to visit me at school, her kids in tow.

"You saved my life," she said. "You know that, don't you? You didn't give up on me when a lot of other people did."

I smiled and gave her half my sandwich. Her dark hair was parted down the middle, and a few freckles were scattered across her Roman nose.

THERE ARE MANY other stories I could tell of true triumph at Central. I wasn't a one-woman army by any means. There were lots of great teachers, administrators, and parents involved, people who cared, helped, and served. In addition to Angie, I had a lot of other kids come work for me over the years, kids I wanted to keep a close eye on. I had the punks, the gangbangers, the misfits, the tough girls, the fat kids, the kids in wheelchairs, the blind kid, the kid whose mother died, the kids who got pregnant, the kids who had abortions, the kids who had a baby their freshman year and another their sophomore year and another their junior year and another their senior, the kids who sold drugs, the kids who overdosed from drugs, and the kids who quit drugs for good.

In the 25 years I worked at the school, the health services climate at Central High School improved tremendously from its beginnings in a small, dark office. The nursing role for me yielded some enormous rays of light. Eventually, I was able to start three new programs at Central. It wasn't all my doing, of course, but I initiated them. I was really proud of those. One was simply named the School Health Center, but it was no small program. It was an actual, full-fledged doctor's office within the school, the only one of its type in the whole state of Rhode Island at the time. A doctor came to the school five days a week to work at the center. I also had a nurse-practitioner and an obstetrician/gynecologist on regular rotation. Before the center began, kids would come to me in need of a doctor's services—they'd have a bad cold, or they'd be pregnant, or they'd be roughed up badly from a fight—but because of their families' income levels, they could only go to the emergency room after school at best; at worst, they'd receive no medical help at all outside what I could do for them at school. So with the center, the kids could see a doctor right on campus, then head back to class or go home with a guardian's permission. Students were able to come to the center for free. The program was funded through the Rhode Island Department of Health, although we billed private insurance companies whenever possible.

Second, we started New Directions, a program for pregnant teens. Doctors from the Women & Infants' Hospital in cooperation with the Department of Human Services provided prenatal care, health education, and parenting advice for kids at the school. Nobody ever wanted to admit that kids were sexually active, but we couldn't ignore the facts. Kids at our school—lots of them—were having babies. Principal Zarrella was a strong proponent of the New Directions program, although other school administrators criticized it openly. "Just tell them to keep their legs closed," one said to me. I explained to her that I preferred that high school kids wouldn't be sexually active in the first place, but if a kid was already pregnant, then she needed help.

Third, we began a day care in our school. Again, critics chimed in, saying that the program made it too easy for teenage girls to have babies—if such a thing was even possible. As before,

I maintained that facts were facts. We had many students who had babies, and the young mothers often had to drop out. There were seldom any fathers involved in raising the babies. Sometimes the extended families helped, but the mothers got part-time jobs if they could or, more often, went on welfare; most never finished school. Our program, the John Hope Day Care, was an offshoot of the John Hope Settlement House. Mornings, kids would drop off their babies. At lunch, they were allowed to come down and feed them. Other than that, they needed to stay in class and focus on their studies. A lot of girls were able to graduate this way.

So I stayed busy, as busy as I could. And I loved it at Central. It was everything my mother said it would be. But even all that, as good as it was, wasn't quite enough for me. As if coordinating these programs, fulfilling my responsibilities as a school nurse, going to kids' sports programs after school, and trying to have a social life all weren't enough for me to do, I started something else, too.

I got a second full-time job.

❖

CHAPTER 8

A Different Type of Craziness

I T WASN'T AS BAD as it sounded. In fact, it wasn't bad at all. I loved my job at Central. I was always on my feet, always busy with kids, always up and on the go. In many ways, being a school nurse didn't feel like work to me. It was just something I loved to do.

For social life, I spent time with my family and friends. There were no serious guys in my life during those years. At first I rented an apartment alone downtown, but after a while I decided to move back home with my parents. I missed living at home. I had my own familiar bedroom there. My mother cooked for me. It was a matter of convenience as much as anything. That, and security.

Donna and I kept in touch constantly. We talked three or four times a day on the phone. She broke up with Marcello after a few additional months in the Peace Corps and came home after that. A short time later, she met a guy named Joe on a ski slope; they got married and had a son, Christopher, a cute redhead. Christopher was a wonderful little hellion from day one, always on the go. He dreamed of being a soldier for as long as anyone could remember. Young Christopher Manion. Remember that name.

Everybody I knew was getting married. My friend from high school, Linda Pezza, got married to Bob, and they had three kids.

Janie Varnum, another good friend from school, got married to Harry, and they had two sons. My sister, Ellen-Ann, and her husband had four children fairly soon in their marriage.

I became the friendly auntie to my sister's and brother's children as well as to all my friends' kids. I went to all their baptisms, their confirmations, their first communions. I was like the neighborhood cat lady, always by herself and always up to something, except I didn't have any cats.

It wasn't that I couldn't get married. I'm sure there would have been boyfriends again, but I just wasn't looking for love. I was looking the other way, actually—completely focused on my job. I'm pretty sure I was reasonably attractive. My weight went back up to about 170 after I started at Central, but I quickly got it down to about 130 from all the running around and was able to maintain that fairly consistently for the next chunk of time. I wanted to be a positive role model and have kids see that I cared about my health. I feared being seen as someone—a fat school nurse—who preached healthy habits but didn't practice them herself.

What really tipped the balance for me, jobwise, was the desire to become the best auntie I could be. My aunt Mary and my uncle Bill had helped put me and my siblings through college. If it hadn't been for the money they sent us, I doubt if we would have been able to afford postsecondary education. So I wanted to make some extra money for my nieces and nephews. More work wasn't a problem. I thrived whenever I worked. For a while, I taught community college a couple of nights a week, but then I started looking for something more permanent.

Back at university I had done my psych practicum at the Institute of Mental Health. People's minds fascinated me. Maybe it was the experience of growing up looking after my aunt Ellen for all those years. So I got a second job at the institute, located in

Cranston. From 8:15 A.M. to 2:45 P.M. I worked at Central High School. Then I zipped over to Cranston and worked from 3:00 to 11:30 P.M. at the institute. I wasn't getting much sleep, but that didn't bother me. Mom provided my meals. Dad provided the roof over my head. Pretty much all I needed to do was work and save money and phone friends. That became my life.

The institute had three sections housed in one complex: the psychiatric unit, the psychiatric hospital, and the psychiatric prison. I worked in the prison. My specific job title was head nurse of the forensic unit, the criminally insane ward. It's where people went when they committed crimes but couldn't go to prison because of mental health issues. They couldn't be sent to a regular mental health unit either, because crimes had been done. We gave patients their meds and looked after as many of their daily functions as necessary, provided counsel when needed, used restraints when we had to, and put people in the seclusion room if they acted out. It was all part of the job. I always tried to be as gentle and respectful of the patients as I could.

The old brick building, with its locked wards, was a bit scary at first glance. Some patients had been there for years. Some came for a night and were transferred elsewhere within 24 hours. Some were allowed to walk around; others weren't. The criminally insane ward was isolated from the other wards, surrounded by a big fence. To get to work, I needed to ring a bell and be let in by a guard. Inside, bedrooms faced each side of a hall, with my office at the end. Several attendants worked alongside of me, all trained in mental health. A psychiatrist was also there regularly. He did the evaluations to determine if people were fit to stand trial. About 20 patients, all men, were on my ward at any given time. It was a high-security place, guarded night and day, but still there were regular squabbles and even occasional fights in the ward. We didn't keep the patients locked in their rooms, and whenever people socialize, particularly in clinical situations such as this, disagreements tend to break out. All my patients were there because they were considered either permanently out of their minds or temporarily insane at the time during which they committed a crime. Some appeared and acted as normal as you or me but had simply been off their medications when they committed their crimes. Once they had been arrested, they got back on their meds and again appeared and acted normal. Still, crimes had been committed, so things were different for them now.

One of my patients, Mister Hwang, liked to draw and paint pictures. He was one of the older patients in the forensic unit, maybe 60, although it was hard to tell his exact age. He had long laugh lines that stretched from underneath his eyes down around the sides of his face to his chin. He wore thick black-framed glasses and often sat studying his easel while holding a paintbrush in his mouth like a thin unlit cigar.

"I like you, Miss Corry . . . Miss Corry, Miss Corry," Mister Hwang said to me one day.

He repeated my name not suggestively, but rather more like a grandfather might talk to his granddaughter. I could tell he was rolling it around in his mind.

"Miss Corry—what does your name mean, do you know?" Mister Hwang asked.

"Uh, it's Irish." I gave him his medication. He drank down the pills with a half glass of water. "I think a corry is a mountain dell. Why do you ask?"

"Mountain dell. There is much honor in a name like that. Names mean much where I come from. I did business with a Mister Wu once. His name meant 'darkness.' He was a man of many shadows."

I tucked in the corners of the blanket that was around Mister Hwang's legs. He often said he was cold, even on warm days. "What does your name mean?" I asked.

"Mister Hwang means 'the man of yellow.'"

"Is that why you like to paint?"

He removed his paintbrush from his mouth and held it out to me as a professor might hold a pointer. "In your country, a man who is yellow is said to be a coward." He said the words slowly, the slightest hint of provocation in his voice. "Perhaps that is what I am."

I smoothed the sweater that covered his shoulders. "No one I know calls you a coward, Mister Hwang."

"There is also the yellow birch, the yellowhammer, the yellow taxicab, and yellowcake, one of the essential ingredients for creating nuclear weapons. Furthermore, there is the yellow submarine, the yellow jersey in bicycling, and, yes, yellow ocher for painting." He returned his paintbrush to his mouth.

"So which are you, Mister Hwang?"

He exhaled slowly. "Yellow was the color of the New Party in Taiwan. We supported the Chinese reunification." Here he paused as if on purpose, as if he was used to keeping his words in check. "No, Miss Corry, I was a cook, a simple cook. I worked in a restaurant and made a yellow mustard sauce. People considered it excellent mustard sauce. I made the sauce like my father made it before me, like his father made it before him, for as many generations as we can remember. That is why I am a man of yellow." He resumed his painting. The conversation was over. He grew engrossed in his work immediately, as if I had suddenly disappeared from the room.

"Mustard sauce, my eye," whispered one of the attendants later. "Mister Hwang was no simple cook. He's a judan, a tenth-degree black belt. He could snap your neck like a twig if he flexed his pinkie. Do you know why he's in here? One day he was in his restaurant and supposedly off his meds. He murdered eight customers in an afternoon. Shot 'em all with a handgun. One of the ladies was pregnant. He could take us all out if he wanted to." The attendant let out a sharp gasp as if picturing the incident.

"He said he wants to draw me a picture," I said. "What do you make of that?"

"I'd say let him. Just keep giving him his meds and let him do anything he wants."

Forensic medicine can be a funny thing. As I made my rounds each evening in the prison unit of the psych ward, I didn't doubt that some of the people there were truly evil, regardless of sanity or any lack thereof. One of my patients had raped a little boy, then chopped him up and eaten his bones. He wasn't in the ward long. When the other patients found out about it, rumors spread that they were going to take him out. Prison can have a very black-and-white justice system within its bars. The man was soon transferred to another facility.

Another man came to us after having sex with an infant. He tore her apart so badly that she needed a colostomy. He was only in the ward for a night before they deemed him fit to stand trial. He went straight to jail. I never heard what happened to him there.

Another patient, Bryce, was a really handsome kid with a shock of shaggy hair and a cool, permanent two-day stubble on his chin. He came from a wonderful family. His father was a doctor and his mother an attorney, just like in the *Cosby Show*. But one day Bryce slit the throat of another guy at a bar. Bryce worked at the bar part-time while studying for his MBA. He went in the back to restock something, and when he came out he had killed someone. As simple as that. Anyone who talked to this kid would never think he was sick in the head.

That was the mystery of the prison unit. Some of my patients genuinely had not wanted to commit a crime or had not thought things out beforehand. Their minds simply didn't work right. Others had sound minds but just did things that were judged insane. The first type of patient was always harder to process. Take a normally healthy person, let his mind go for whatever reason, and sometimes the results were tragic.

Once, an elderly man was brought to the ward for evaluation. He had committed some local crime, robbed a store or something. He wore a cardigan sweater and looked so frail that I doubted he was much of an actual threat. His arms were quivering, even handcuffed as he was. He kept hopping from one foot to the next, groaning and wincing as if it took all his muscular effort to hop. It wasn't the sort of activity a person would choose to do. The police took him to jail and then brought him to us until they sorted out their next steps.

"I don't like that old man," Bryce said to me. His two-day stubble was perfect as he brushed the shock of hair from his eyes. "He keeps moving all over. I think he's trying to touch me."

"Stay away from him, then." I eyed Bryce closely. "The man's not going to be here long."

"I don't like him at all," Bryce went on. "I don't like him one bit. He keeps staring at me. I think he's out to get me."

"He's not out to get you, Bryce. No one's out to get you here."

That weekend I needed to be out of town for something and couldn't be on duty. But I took Bryce's complaints about the old man seriously. A person's anxieties are valid; even if he is crazy, the anxieties are real in his mind. I instructed the weekend staff to keep an eye on the elderly man and to make sure Bryce stayed away from him at all times.

On Monday when I returned, however, I was shocked to learn

that the elderly man was dead. It had happened in a heartbeat. Someone wasn't looking. Bryce slipped out of his room and strangled the man. We ordered a full investigation at once. Later, we found out the additional tragedy. The autopsy showed that the elderly man had a degenerative brain disease. He shouldn't even have been sent to us—not even for the alleged crime he was charged with. There was no way for authorities to assess his condition that quickly, so the ward was technically deemed not responsible for the man's death. Still, the whole situation was heartbreaking. He could have been anyone's grandfather whose mind had just happened to slip. An unbalanced mind led him to commit a small crime, the crime led him to the institute, and his placement there led to his death.

Those were the stakes of our job. It was a mixed world where evil and good and mistakes and crimes and innocence and guilt were all rolled into one. Another nurse was grabbed from behind one night by one of the patients. He would have broken her neck, but others intervened quickly. The nurse quit. I didn't blame her. Another patient came to us for a minor crime, I don't even remember what. He seemed like the sweetest guy. We got his medications regulated. He passed all his psychological exams. He was released and a day later went out and murdered his mother. Such high-stakes uncertainty was the different type of craziness we faced on a regular basis.

"Miss Corry, I painted this picture for you," Mister Hwang said late one December. "It is for your Christmastime. You Christians, yes—this is your holiday."

I held the card close to me. Mister Hwang had painted a snow-covered hill at night. Seven perfect evergreens dotted the hill. At the top of the hill sat the silhouette of a small city. Bethlehem, I supposed, for above the city Mister Hwang had painted one blazing star of light. Its vertical beam descended all the way to the town.

"It's a beautiful card, Mister Hwang. I'll treasure it always." I opened the card. There was a five-dollar bill inside. That was a lot of money for a patient to have on him in the early 1980s.

"Your tip," he said. "You're a good worker, Miss Corry. I like you. I like your name. Mountain dell. Me, I am the man of yellow." His voice was quiet but firm. As he talked he held his paintbrush in his mouth.

I decided it was an appropriate gift from a former restaurant worker turned artist. I couldn't keep his money, of course. It was against policy, and I wouldn't have wanted to anyway. I applied it back on his account so that he would still feel honored by giving the gift.

SOMETIMES IT WAS very hard to tell where the line was drawn between sane and insane. It was like that at my school job, too, but in a different way.

My colleague and good friend Jackie taught business courses at Central until she became pregnant with her fourth child and transferred to an elementary school. One day she came back to Central to visit me. It was lunchtime and we were in my office enjoying sandwiches, coffee, and doughnuts when we heard yelling in Spanish outside followed by a quick *bang, bang, bang*. Jackie's eyes were big. "It sounds like someone's throwing something at the school," she said.

"Get down quick," I ordered. "Those are gunshots."

The shots were over in a minute, and we got up to peer out the window. Everything looked strangely clear. As we headed out to check on things, a girl came down the hallway toward us, wincing with every step. "Somebody threw a rock at my back," she said. "It's killing me."

"Inside—quick!" I said, and took her arm. I knew it was no

rock. The girl gasped for breath. The large veins in her neck stuck out. They were turning blue from lack of oxygen. Her pulse was rapid. Her blood pressure was decreasing. Her lungs were starting to collapse. Jackie dialed 911. "You just stay with me, okay?" I said to the girl. I hoped my voice wasn't shaking. "You're going to be all right—you hear? You're going to be fine." There was no way of telling how deep the bullet had gone, or what other damage had been done. I had seen a lot of gunshot wounds back in Brazil. Bullets are unpredictable. They can bounce around inside a person and damage a lot of tissue, ribs, and major organs. I worked to control the bleeding from the girl's back.

As I worked, my thoughts strayed to evil and innocence and how they often collided: the serenity of Mister Hwang's Christmas picture with the stories of what he had done; the birth of Christ in a manger with the Massacre of the Innocents; this crimeless schoolgirl with a random bullet. Would the scarred world of King Herod always need to be dealt with?

"It really hurts." The girl panted. She was getting shorter of breath. Suddenly, there was no sound at all. I tilted her head back, pinched her nose, and gave two quick breaths. No air. Nothing.

"Jackie—those paramedics need to get here quick!" I said. I carefully pushed down on the girl's chest, counted to 30, then gave two more quick breaths.

One other kid had been shot that day. He staggered into my office just as the paramedics arrived. He had been shot in the leg but not seriously hurt. Apparently a gang from Massachusetts had a beef with a gang from Providence. Some of that gang's kids went to Central, so the Massachusetts gang had driven by the school and fired indiscriminately into the schoolyard. It was a miracle that more people didn't get shot.

The girl who thought she'd been hit by a rock was taken to the hospital, and later we learned that she would pull through.

But that wasn't the end of the day's excitement. Later that afternoon, the science teacher ran into my office. His arm was bleeding. "Help!" he cried. "I've been bitten by a shark."

"What?" I said, and jumped up to look at his arm.

"I'm serious. I keep a huge stuffed shark hanging on my wall. In the middle of class it fell off and sliced my arm. I think I need stitches." Despite his pain, he was trying hard not to laugh.

"You're going to need some stitches all right," I said, examining the wound. "One thing's for sure. I've seen a lot of nutso things in this job, but you're the only person I know who can say he's been attacked by a shark at school."

We were both laughing now.

At least we could recognize this kind of craziness for what it was.

CHAPTER 9

Love, in a Dangerous Time

THE BUMS USED TO hang out across the street from Central High School. That's what everybody called them back then. There was a YMCA on the corner, and most mornings you saw homeless men milling about or flopped on the sidewalk in front of it. Sometimes they were sleeping there. Sometimes they had collapsed and were struggling to get back up. I received a number of calls due to situations like that. People in the neighborhood got to know me and knew my position. Somehow, I became the de facto neighborhood nurse to the homeless men at the Y.

One morning, I received a call about a man who had collapsed on the sidewalk and appeared unconscious. Principal Zarrella and I went out to take a look. It was winter and cold, and on his head the homeless man wore a tattered blue stocking cap with a red stripe around it. It looked like it had been a jaunty hat once. Perhaps a young grandson had picked it out for him years ago as a gift. But it was hard to gauge the passage of time with the homeless. The man might have been 80 or he might have been 60. He was dirty and unshaven and had vomited whiskey all over the front of his overcoat. Underneath his coat, he wore a frayed dress shirt buttoned high and tight around his neck, like he had really been working hard to keep out the cold. Someone from the Y came out and said that she had seen him walking around for a few days, and that the old man had stayed at least one night at the Y. Although he was still warm, the man was not breathing and had no pulse. Principal Zarrella immediately began chest compressions.

"You want my handkerchief?" he said. "You're the nurse."

"Yeah, thanks, Arthur," I said. That meant I was the one who needed to perform mouth-to-mouth. I wiped away the vomit as best as I could and blew in two short breaths. My blowing made a sound like a vacuum cleaner clogged with lint. "Something funny's going on here. I can't get any air in."

"Doesn't look like he's got much food left in him," Principal Zarrella said. "His tongue's stuck, maybe? Or maybe he choked on his vomit."

"Can't find anything in his mouth." I probed with my fingers. "Maybe it's a blockage farther down."

Principal Zarrella reached to undo the man's top buttons. He paused. "Hey, Sue, you'll wanna see this."

Plastic tubing ran around the man's neck, with a small opening in front. The man had a tracheotomy. No wonder I couldn't get any air in. I removed the inner cannula from the trach and gave two gentle puffs into the tube. Air was getting through now, but there were still no signs of life. We counted off and tried again. Still nothing. About a minute went by. Finally, Principal Zarrella said, "I've got a little pulse." We kept up with the procedure. Then, just as the ambulance pulled up, the old man gave a little start and coughed. He remained unconscious, or so we thought—his eyes never opened and he didn't respond to repeated questions we asked—but at least he was breathing on his own again. The paramedics set up their equipment and took over; the old man went to the hospital. Principal Zarrella and I both went back to the school.

The story was over, or so we thought. It was just another average day at Central for us, but about a year later I received a strange letter at school. "Greetings," it began. "You are hereby ordered to appear and give testimony . . ." It was a subpoena.

And there was more.

The old man was not a bum at all. He was homeless, yes, but only temporarily, or so his family claimed. He had been a wealthy businessman for years and still owned homes and land and had "only recently gone off his rocker," one of his family members mumbled when I met them in the attorney's office.

The old man's attorney filled in the details. The man Principal Zarrella and I had revived on the street did in fact die, but not until two weeks later. A lot happened between the time we saw the paramedics put him in the ambulance and when he breathed his last. The paramedics had taken him to the hospital, where he was asked the standard questions: "Who's your nearest relative? Who do you know who might live nearby?" He had no identification on him. No address card.

"I know Sue, the school nurse at Central," the man said. "She saved my life."

It was no mindless croaking out a name. Apparently not to him, anyway, for the old man had called his attorney and changed his will, right then and there in the hospital. The attorney, at least, believed the old man was of sound mind. And the man's estate went to me.

I was rich. The man had left it all, or at least a sizable sum, to the nurse he believed had stopped on the street to save his life. That's what the family was contesting, and that's what the subpoena was about.

Who was I, some money-grabbing nurse who filled their dear, sweet old grandfather with lies on his deathbed? Who was I, some meddling outsider who tricked a poor, innocent elderly father into thinking I was his rescuer? Our dear father was deluded, swayed by gratitude, they said. It must have been a moment of misguided emotion, for surely he would never do anything so heartless as to forget his own family.

I didn't fight. The act of changing the will was a sweet gesture on the old man's part, but I didn't want his money. Certainly not like that. He had a family, even if he didn't like them much, or even if they let him wander around city streets and sleep at the Y. Someone had once given him that jaunty blue stocking cap with the red stripe. The money needed to go to them. I withdrew from the will's ruling and didn't take a dime.

THAT HAPPENED IN the early 1980s. I sometimes wonder what would have happened if I had taken the man's money. Would a sudden influx of money have changed my life? I wasn't looking for a change; I liked the direction I was going. But two other things happened in the early 1980s that did change my life.

The birth of a baby is a wonderful thing. As a nurse, I had witnessed many births when I was in Brazil. My sister, Ellen-Ann, and her husband, Steve Higginbotham, had already produced two beautiful baby girls, Katie and Meg. The girls were healthy and perfect, and I fell in love with them each time I saw them. When their brother, my nephew, Geoffrey, was born in 1983, everything seemed okay. There were balloons and snuggly blankets and shower gifts and lots of celebrating. But as the weeks continued, something seemed a little off.

Right around then my brother, Jackie, and his wife, Toni, also gave birth to a son, John Patrick, who was big and healthy. Compared with John Patrick side by side, Geoffrey seemed so much smaller. Geoffrey was never much of an eater. Give him a bottle and he'd scrunch up his nose and wail as the fluid went down, as if his stomach was in great pain. Doctors ran a series of tests but didn't seem to find anything wrong.

Finally, after several weeks of uncertainty, the doctors performed a sweat test, which checks for abnormal amounts of sodium and chloride in a person's body. The results came back conclusive: Geoffrey had cystic fibrosis (CF). Our family was devastated, of course. At the time, kids diagnosed with CF had a life expectancy of 12 years at most. With the onset of better meds and treatments in the years since, that number has been upped to 37 years, but it's still a terminal disease no matter how you look at it. There is no known cure. CF is primarily a lung and digestive disease, although it affects the liver, pancreas, and intestines as well. With CF, a person's mucus glands don't function properly. The disease eventually shuts down a variety of the body's systems and causes progressive disability, then death. A child with CF often has a hard time breathing and eating. After the diagnosis, Geoffrey needed to chew about ten big pills before he ate, or else he couldn't digest anything and would get violent stomachaches.

Our whole family was at risk, really. It's a hereditary disease caused from a recessive gene. My mother had a brother, Jack, who died at age 11. He was always sickly and never could breathe right. Back in the 1920s, they didn't diagnose CF like they do now, and no one knew the disease ran in our family. Even today, with the recessive gene pinpointed, it's sort of like a huge genetic crapshoot. The disease won't always occur in a child when the parents carry the gene. Ellen-Ann and Steve's two girls are fine. But a few years later, my sister and her husband gave birth to another boy, Matthew, who was also diagnosed with CF. Just before then, my brother Jackie and his wife had a boy, Ryan, and his test came back positive, too. Little Mary came along later, but she was fine.

So that meant I soon had three nephews, all with CF: Geoffrey, Matthew, and Ryan. Kids with CF spend a lot of the time in the hospital. Our family has come to call it going in for tune-ups. These kids need a lot of equipment and medicines just to be able to breathe. Home medicine cabinets become like little pharmacies. I glimpsed this expensive future and made up my mind. I loved my nephews like I would love children of my own, and I decided that my life would be dedicated to helping take care of them. If they weren't going to live long, then at least the lives they would lead would be great ones. I was positive I would never get married. My life would be dedicated to working two full-time jobs for as long as I was able and being the unencumbered relative who could dig in and serve.

That thought was still in my mind one day in December 1984. I was 34 years old, the hardworking unmarried auntie, but that day would begin the second thing that changed my life. A man named Albert Miller worked the first shift at the Institute of Mental Health. I worked second shift, but Albert and I always saw each other at changeover and said hello. He knew I was single. His wife, Lana, had a brother, George Luz, who lived in California and had just come home to Rhode Island to visit for a few weeks. Albert wondered if I was interested in going on a blind date with George while he was here.

No way, I thought. To begin with, the guy was six and a half years younger than I was. He was some actor or something, or at least that was why he was in California—he was trying to make it in Hollywood. On the side he was selling fire extinguishers. *A salesman/struggling actor? Hoo boy, what a winning combination,* I thought. What I didn't know at the time was that George wasn't particularly interested in going on any blind dates either. He had asked Albert if he knew anyone who might need a fire extinguisher. Albert had said something like, "Yeah, I know this gal at work who might need one." George had strictly commercial interests on the brain.

I'm not positive how Albert convinced me to agree to a date with George. I remember saying I wasn't going to go out to a restaurant with him or anything. George and I could meet on my lunch hour at school. I only had half an hour for lunch, actually, not even a full hour, so I figured if I didn't like the guy I could ditch him pretty quick.

When I first saw George Luz, I remember thinking I wasn't too impressed. George was Portuguese and skinny, maybe 150 pounds. If a relationship with him ever took off and I gained any weight, I'd dwarf him. It was raining that day; he wore a dark raincoat and carried a briefcase with a fire extinguisher inside. Poor guy—he really did meet me only to make a sale. It was certainly not love at first sight, at least as far as I was concerned.

We went to lunch in the most unromantic place I could think of: Central's vocational building. They had a culinary school there. We each had a sandwich. George explained how he demonstrated the fire extinguishers by setting his briefcase on fire and then putting it out. I was briefly called to the office for something, and when I came back George had made great friends with Joe Trombetta, the principal of the voc school, and set his briefcase on fire to show Joe.

What a nut, I thought. Yet while George doused the flames, Joe, always the direct sort, sidled up to me and said, "This guy's all right, you know. You should settle down with him, Sue."

But I was already convinced that George wasn't my type. I bought a fire extinguisher from him out of pity; I hoped that a sale would get rid of him. So I was surprised a day later when he phoned me up and asked me to lunch again. I said no, but he phoned again. I said no again. He persisted. In fact, he upped his pitch and asked me out for dinner. Was this guy loony? The only time I had for dinner was my dinner break during my shift at the prison. He'd need to come there. How many men would come down to the forensic unit to take a girl out on a date? He came.

A funny thing began to happen. The more George and I talked, the more he surprised me. There was something calming about him, something stable in his demeanor. He had a great sense of humor. He listened well. He was even okay-looking when I eyed him closely. We went to a few football games at Central. I asked him to chaperone a prom with me (hey—I had to dance with somebody). Zarrella liked him, Trombetta liked him—both men whose opinions I respected.

Then George came over and met my family, and my mother absolutely flipped. By that time *anyone* who dated her 35-year-old single daughter was wonderful in her eyes. George and my dad smoked cigarettes and drank soda in the living room. George rented a couple of videos and showed scenes from a couple of the movies he had been in: *The Star Maker* with Rock Hudson, Suzannne Pleshette, and Melanie Griffith, and *Body and Soul* with Muhammad Ali and Jayne Kennedy. "All screwball movies," George called them. I could tell he didn't take himself too seriously; that was a good sign.

While George was out of the room, my father turned to us and quipped, "He better not give up his day job, because he's never going to make it as an actor." That was just the way Daddy was. I could tell he really liked him, too. He flipped on the TV to *Hawaii 5-0* and smoked another cigarette before George came back.

It wasn't head-spinning love, not yet anyway, but I liked being around George, I really did. He had grown up in West Warwick, only about 20 minutes from Providence, so he knew all the same places I did. And . . . he was interested in me—I couldn't quite figure that one out. We were opposites on so many levels. He loved sports and California. I hated to run and wanted to travel the world and take care of my nieces and nephews. He had told me that he really liked the rapport I had with my students, the way I talked to them, the concern I showed for them. Maybe he saw my character for what it was. Or—who knows?—maybe I was just on my best behavior.

Right around then, I splurged and bought myself a new VW convertible. It was a great car, the only new car I had ever owned, and I wanted a reliable car for the commutes I was making to both my jobs. I loved the way the VW felt when the top was down and I was driving with the wind in my hair. But shortly after the purchase, the car was stolen. Both of my jobs were in bad areas of town, and cars were always getting broken into or getting their windows shot out. So I bought another VW Beetle, although this one was just a dented old beater to get me around. The second car was on a quick path to its final destination in the junkyard. George offered to take me car shopping for a better one. It sounded like a good date, so we went and I fell in love with a little beige BMW 325 at the dealer. It was used but still in great condition. We walked away. I wanted some time to think about it. That was the way I worked best.

A few weeks passed and it was mid-February, right around Valentine's Day. Thoughts of cupids and chocolate filled the air. We had been dating for about ten weeks by then, and George picked me up on my lunch hour from Central. It didn't dawn on me at first what had taken place.

"Hey, you bought yourself that car we looked at," I said. He was driving the little beige BMW we had seen together.

"Yeah, okay, something like that," he said. "Actually, I bought the car for you."

"What? George, are you kidding?"

"No, it's for real. And there's something more, too. Get in and I'll tell you about it." Something about the tone of his voice made me shut up and not ask any more questions. We got in and headed up Route 95. He cleared his throat. Traffic was light and we breezed along. "Sue, take a look in the glove compartment. There's something in there I want you to see."

I looked inside. It was one of those moments you just don't see coming. Within the glove compartment was a tiny velvet box. Inside the box was an emerald ring with diamonds all around it.

"It was your grandmother's ring," George said. "Your mother gave it to me. I had them put it in a new setting."

"It's beautiful," I said.

He cleared his throat again. Apparently, there was no stopping the man. "Will you marry me, Susan Corry?" he asked. The traffic zipped by us. We were in the slow lane now.

I looked at the ring. I looked at the man beside me. I looked ahead at the freeway. "Okay, George," I said.

My response was as straightforward as that. Saying yes felt like the logical thing to do. I was starting to fall in love with him; I doubt if I was truly there yet, but I figured if I was ever going to get married, it would need to be now or never. I was content with never, but I knew George would make a good husband. So why not? Not much else in my life would need to change—at least that's what I told myself there on the freeway. We probably wouldn't have children of our own; we had talked about my situation earlier. I would still keep both my jobs and work crazy hours. My parents were always going to be very close to me. I'd keep all my same friends. George would just need to fit into my life. That was the deal as I saw it.

George's resolve was tested fairly early in our engagement.

An incident happened that showed him what he was getting into. There was a McDonald's across the street from Central High School. Kids weren't allowed to go there, but they went anyway. George came to school to take me to lunch one day, and we went to a Dunkin' Donuts right down from the McDonald's. As we were eating, we heard a *bang, bang, bang*—really loud.

"George, that's gunfire!" I said. We ran toward the sound. A crowd was starting to gather at the McDonald's. We got there at the same time Principal Zarrella arrived. I feared the worst.

It was a horrible sight. A boy was lying in the parking lot, a large dark pool of blood underneath him. He had been shot in the stomach. A troubled high school kid we all knew had blown away the first boy with a shotgun. The troubled kid had just recently dropped out of school, but he had come back to campus to settle some gang-related score.

"We've got to give him CPR!" Principal Zarrella yelled.

I shook my head. I knew without a doubt the boy was already gone. "No," I said softly. "He's not coming back." He had been hit with a shotgun blast; his intestines were completely blown away.

It was an awful day, a tragic waste of life. It shook up not only the school but also the whole city, judging by the tone and frequency of the news reports. Principal Zarrella was called to testify at the hearing. He had been closer to the scene of the crime than I had—that time anyway. Later, George and I talked about the incident in depth. The shooting of a student was heartbreaking enough, but the incident raised other issues, issues that we had to face together now. What if we had been sitting at the McDonald's instead of the Dunkin' Donuts? What if a shotgun blast had mistakenly headed our direction? What if that had been one of us lying on the ground with our intestines spilled all over? These were the harsh realities of what I did for a living. I worked in a war zone—two of them, actually. "Sue, I'm not going to try to stop you from working either of your jobs," George said. "I worry about you, yes, about the places you work and the schedule you keep, but I know you're needed in these places. You've got my support."

So that was what I needed to know. Things were set.

We wanted to get married that summer, but it wasn't until April that we started planning our wedding. We were supposed to take premarital classes from Sacred Heart Church, where we wanted the ceremony to be performed, but when we went down there the priest said, "Ah, Sue Corry, I've known your mother for years. If you're anything like her, and I know you are, then you don't need to take any marriage classes." George was all too happy to get out of the lessons. He's a smart guy but self-admittedly not much of a studier. He reads books only when on airplanes.

I wrote a letter to the Squantum Club, one of Rhode Island's most famous wedding venues. You had to be a member of the club or know someone there to get a booking. We weren't members, but they recognized my family's name as longtime area residents, so we were able to put a date on the calendar for the reception as long as it would be held on a Sunday. Everybody else in Rhode Island had spent a long time planning their wedding, I guess, because all the Saturdays at the Squantum Club were booked for years in advance. That was okay by me. The Squantum Club has beautiful lawns that overlook a rocky coastline and a main clubhouse porch where beautiful pictures can be taken at sunset. I went in to their administrative office and planned the wedding within two hours. They provided a five-piece orchestra. I didn't want anything huge, no sit-down dinner or anything, just champagne and a buffet table with hors d'oeuvres. The wedding planned, George and I got into our first fight. It was a squabble really, a small tiff. I wanted only a hundred people at the reception. It needed to be small and private, just family and friends. But George comes from a huge family. Each of his parents has a dozen brothers and sisters. But we could only invite 50 people each. We worked it out.

The night before the wedding, we held the rehearsal dinner at George's mom's house. My folks and his folks had met once or twice previously. Things went smoothly, but on the way back home in the car I started wondering. What was I doing anyway, getting married? Marriage wasn't supposed to be in the cards for me. I was in the backseat with my mother and my aunt Mary. My father was driving and my sister was in the other front seat.

"Y'know, Ma," I said, "I don't know if I really want to get married after all."

"What?" My sister craned her head around from the front. "Of course you're getting married. Don't even think such a thing. George is a wonderful man. You need to be happy and settle down."

"She don't need to marry no Portagee if she don't want to." That was my father growling from the driver's seat, always the Archie Bunker character.

"Maybe I'll just get married and try it out for a while," I said. "I can always get divorced if things don't work out."

"Susan! Really!" That was my mother. She made the sign of the cross. "You can never get divorced. You can't even be thinking that. Particularly on the night before you get married."

"It's just the jitters," said my sister.

"Yes, that's all it is. Nerves," said my mother. "We're all just a little bit nervous."

"Well, I ain't," said my dad. "You just make sure he doesn't quit his day job."

George and I were married August 25, 1985. It rained on our wedding day—a nonstop torrential downpour. We were married at Sacred Heart Church, then we headed over to the Squantum Club for the reception. I threw the bouquet from the stairs. We cut the cake. It was a beautiful wedding. Small, private, only a hundred people to witness the day with us. The only time it stopped pouring was during pictures. The sky opened up, the sun came out, we took pictures, and then it started pouring again. That's supposed to be good luck if it rains on the wedding day—you have rain then, but sunshine forever after.

For our honeymoon, George and I flew to Bermuda. We stayed at the Hamilton Princess Hotel. The sunsets stretched to infinity, filling each night's sky with reds, oranges, indigos, and purples. Everything was so romantic, so perfect. We took long walks on the beach. We lay in the sun. We sipped cool drinks by the pool. I never thought this whole experience could be possible. I was truly married, and to a truly great man. I telephoned my mother from Bermuda. "I think I'm really in love," I said.

George had given up acting and the fire extinguisher business and had received his real estate license a short time before the wedding. Right before we were married, he found this great little two-bedroom house for us in Chepachet, a small town near Providence. It had a little fireplace and a cozy little backyard. From the windows, we could see nearby Keech Pond. We bought it for $60,000. George's sister, Lana, lived nearby. George and I didn't live together beforehand. Both my parents and his would have flipped. I had some out-of-town business when the sale went through and never even saw the inside of the house until after we were married. But I loved our little house. George has great taste.

We settled into a routine fairly quickly. George sold houses. I worked my two jobs. We saw each other mostly on weekends and late at night. George learned how to cook. Hey, I never knew how—my mother had always cooked for me. Every once in a while, George let it slip that he thought my pace was too much. But this was me, for better or worse. I was busy, busy, busy.

Actually, I worked three jobs, depending on how it was counted. In 1983, two years before George and I were married, I had joined the Army Reserves, which meant additional time away from home. My motivation for joining was simply because it was something I had always wanted to do, even on top of my other jobs. This wasn't college anymore. Now I was an adult, and now I could make my own decisions. Some join the army because they want extra money to pay for school, but I already had my master's degree. Some want extra pay, but I was already working two jobs. The extra pay from the third job was fine by me—it would also go to pay for special things for my nieces and nephews, but what really motivated me was that old fire I felt to serve. Plain and simple, I wanted to do my duty. I wanted to help other people live better lives.

One winter about a year and a half after getting married, I was driving home in my BMW from my shift at the prison late at night. The roads were horrible, snowy, icy. I flipped on the radio long enough to hear we were in the midst of one of the worst ice storms in Rhode Island's history. The road in front of me was dark. Visibility was nonexistent. Ice pellets sounded like tiny bullets hitting the car.

I was about four miles from home still, inching along well below the speed limit, when from out of nowhere a car appeared. His lights were in my rearview mirror. Then he was beside me. *That guy is going way too fast for these conditions,* I thought. *He's really going to hurt someone.* He whipped around in front. As he cut in, the back of his bumper touched the front of mine. That was all my car needed. The back fishtailed; the front drifted to the ditch. I fought the wheel. I touched the brakes, hoping for traction. Nothing was gripping. My car spun off the road, almost in slow motion, and hurtled down a short bank. I was going faster than I thought I'd been. A huge tree appeared in my car's headlights. It loomed up in an instant. *Smash!* Then there was nothing.

There in the dark, I tried to take stock of my surroundings. The bark of a huge tree was right next to me in the passenger seat. My car was T-boned into the tree. *It's a good thing the car hit on that side,* I thought, *because if my driver's door hit, I'd be a goner.* My headlights were flickering. The car's engine was dead. Snow and ice were blowing in from shattered windows. I felt all over, my arms, my legs, my ribs, my collarbone. Something was making me wince, but I couldn't quite pinpoint where the pain was coming from. I figured I'd be bruised all over the next day, at the very least. I tried the ignition. The car wouldn't start. I knew I couldn't drive it anyway, even if it started, but what I was most interested in now was heat. My seat belt was jimmied. I tugged and strained. Nothing was moving.

About ten minutes passed while I tried to figure out a Plan B. All around me was silence. The road was above me. I doubted anyone could see the car. The wind kept blowing icy blasts through the shattered windows. The longer I sat, the colder I felt. I took stock of my situation: There were no cars out on the road. The car that had hit me hadn't stopped. This was a rural area, only a few houses on this road, and they weren't anywhere close. I doubted if anyone else had seen or heard me crash. This time I was the victim, lying injured and helpless, needing someone, and it seemed unlikely that anyone would come. So this was it: I was trapped in my car in the worst ice storm in Rhode Island's history.

I would soon be a Popsicle. All they'd find would be my frozen cadaver the next morning.

An hour passed. The snow continued to fall.

Then two hours. I was really chattering. Someone better come along quick.

Then, finally, "Ma'am! Hey! Is anybody down there? Is everybody all right?"

Thank God! I heard the voice before I saw where it came from. A uniform. From up above. The man was a correctional officer. I recognized him as someone who had worked on the same campus as me.

"Wow, you're really lucky," he yelled over the wind. "No one's out right now. I came home and pulled in my driveway a ways up the road, but this little voice said I should go look in the woods over there. I had no idea why. That's when I saw your car. I just called the state police. They should be here quick. You want me to call you an ambulance, too?"

"No . . . no thanks," I said. I could barely keep it together. The nearest hospital was 30 minutes away on dry roads. It would take us four times that long in this storm. "I'm not going anywhere far tonight. I just want to go home." I was calling the shots on this one.

The police arrived shortly. They called George. He had been frantic not knowing where I was. These were the days before cell phones. He had called the state police, so they were keeping a lookout for any crashed cars. The police took me home. The BMW wasn't going anywhere except to the junkyard. George drove me to the hospital the next day. That's when they discovered I had broken my collarbone.

And that's when George sat me down and said that some things needed to change. Two jobs, plus the reserves. Out all the time, all hours, all kinds of weather. School shootings. Trouble at the prison. I couldn't keep going at this pace. This was no kind of crazy married life to be leading.

It took some convincing, but I realized George was right.

Something needed to go.

❖

CHAPTER 10

Reserve Missions

I KISSED MY HUSBAND. I kissed him softly on the cheek. I knew that George was right. If I was going to make a decision, I needed to make it now, and when I thought it through, even briefly, there was no question in my mind. But familiar habits are seldom changed overnight. There was no great fanfare in saying good-bye. I set the pan of brownies I had just baked on the counter. They were cool now.

"George, you want one of these?" I said. I cut the brownies into squares.

He nodded. "When are you leaving, Susan?"

"This weekend."

He took the brownie. "So soon, already?"

I nodded. I ate a brownie. It was big, moist, and still hot. I drank a glass of milk. George drank some milk, too. I looked at George and covered the remaining brownies. I glanced over to where he was sitting. I might not have been completely head-over-heels in love with him when we got married, but from the wedding day onward, this skinny man had continually captured and held my heart. We were still on our honeymoon—that's what it felt like—even more than a year after being married. When I looked deep into my heart, I knew that my fears in the car the night before our wedding had just been jitters. No, I wouldn't give up George. Not for the sake of my career, not for the sake of my calling.

"George, I've decided. I'm quitting the psych ward. What do you think of that?"

George exhaled and nodded. You could almost hear the tension leave the room. I was just going to the reserves that weekend; I wasn't leaving him. "I think life with you is always going to be a little crazy," he said. "And that's what I love about you, Sue. That's what I think of you quitting the psych ward."

I grinned. George poured us each another glass of milk. We each took another brownie. Then we put the cover back on the pan, a picture of our resolve: to go forward in health, in love with each other, together forever for better or worse.

SOME PEOPLE THINK of the U.S. military and immediately the word "war" comes to mind. But thousands of American troops regularly take part in humanitarian and peacekeeping work around the globe, even with the conflicts in Afghanistan and Iraq continuing. The goal of the noncombatant missions is to help set conditions for stability and economic prosperity in places of political turmoil and in the immediate aftermath of natural disasters. The idea is not a new one. American troops have been undertaking humanitarian and peacekeeping projects for more than a century. The military has done everything from combating yellow fever in Central America, to undertaking massive humanitarian and reconstruction efforts in the grim aftermath of World War II, to setting up and implementing large-scale emergency rescue operations following earthquakes, floods, and hurricanes.

The idea of serving in humanitarian missions beckoned me. As a nurse, though, I wasn't opposed to taking part in a war.

I knew that if my country needed me, I would do whatever was in my power to do. But the larger idea of helping people around the world—that was a huge draw for me. I was motivated to roll up my sleeves, pitch in, and do my part.

The second conversation I had with my father about joining the army proved as straightforward as the first. He was still a man of few words in 1983 when I told him I was joining the reserves. I looked around the kitchen at the familiar chrome toaster, the telephone, the Formica on the kitchen counter, but this time I wasn't right out of college and saying I wanted to go to Vietnam. This time I was an adult, and I wasn't seeking his permission. Yet I was proud of my father, so proud of him always, and I wanted him to be proud of me. I think I was seeking his approval. Perhaps I told him about my decision because I hoped for his blessing.

"You just make sure you always take care of the people under you," my father said. He shifted in his favorite old chair in the kitchen and lit a cigarette. "If you're going to be an army officer, you make sure you're a damn good one."

I nodded.

That was the extent of our conversation.

I was commissioned as a first lieutenant on June 15, 1983. The commitment with the reserves meant I was gone one weekend per month and two weeks per year; I could also choose to go on additional missions. My parents both came down to the reserve center with me. I raised my right hand while standing in front of the flag and took the oath of enlistment:

> I, Susan Corry, do solemnly swear that I will support and defend the Constitution of the United States against all enemies, foreign and domestic; that I will bear true faith and allegiance to the same; and that I will obey the orders

of the President of the United States and the orders of the officers appointed over me, according to regulations and the Uniform Code of Military Justice. So help me God.

It wasn't a big ceremony. Because of my rank, I was sent to basic training for just two weeks. I sweated and grunted with the rest of the recruits and reminded myself that I only needed to pass one physical fitness test per year to stay in the reserves. If I kept my weight down, I knew I could do that.

My first position with the reserves was at Memorial Hospital in Pawtucket, Rhode Island. I worked as a medical-surgical nurse and hated it, but I knew the training was necessary if we ever did go to war. I buckled down and earned additional designations. Soon my military occupation specialty (MOS) was as both a psychiatric nurse and a community health nurse. I made the rank of captain in 1985.

Back in Pawtucket, on my first day on the job, I met Second Lieutenant Elaine D'Antuono. She had reddish-blond hair and was feisty in a good way. She had joined the army in 1981 and was the woman I talked to right before I left for Iraq, the one who told me it was going to be more difficult than I imagined. When we first met, I had rank over her and was technically her boss, but she had the experience and showed me around. We became quick friends. Soon we did our first mission to England together. In a span of three weeks, we set up a medical clinic and made friends with a priest named Father Doran, who knew the area really well and showed us all around whenever we had an off hour. We took the train to London, and I bought a bunch of Christmas presents at the Laura Ashley store. London was a flurry of activity: rain and the Tower Bridge and Buckingham Palace and Westminster Abbey and double-decker buses. The night before returning home, we went off base and went shopping again. Father Doran couldn't go with us this time, and Elaine and I got horribly lost in London. We rode the rails forever. When we finally did get back, I found that someone had stolen all the Christmas presents I'd bought. Sadly, sometimes that happens on a military base. I picked up one ragged ribbon the thief had left behind and felt a dismal disappointment, but at the same time I mentally shrugged.

In 1989, Elaine and I went on a mission to Honduras. We ran a shift at a 20-bed clinic. The line outside the base included people with ulcers on their legs, people with bellies big from worms or malnutrition, pregnant women, people wanting shots. They stood in the sun and few wore shoes. The conditions were similar to what I had seen in the Peace Corps. Danger seemed to lurk behind every tree and around every corner on this mission. An American had recently been beheaded in the city square, nearby the base. We were told to be extremely careful if we ever went beyond the base's walls. Elaine and I went out for coffee early one evening, except that we were told to avoid the coffee because it was often cut with cocaine. As we were sipping sodas, an armed Honduran soldier burst into the restaurant. Elaine stared at him. "Look away," I hissed. "Don't look at him." The soldier glanced around the restaurant with a scowl then left without incident. We were sure he was searching for someone.

As we were heading home from Honduras, our plane was rerouted to El Salvador. There were only about 30 reservists in our group. No one was sure why we had been rerouted. When we landed, the El Salvadorian army came on the plane, rifles drawn, and wanted to know what the American military was doing in their country. They took us off the plane for questioning. Their glances felt sour and menacing. No one seemed to know what was going on. Our commander kept reiterating that we had been on a humanitarian mission. Finally, after about a day, we were back on another plane heading home.

When the first Persian Gulf War broke out in 1991, our unit was activated; some went to the Persian Gulf, and some were sent to Walter Reed Hospital in Washington, D.C. I didn't go to war then. I was classified as backfill, someone who filled in for active-duty personnel when they needed a vacation or went off to war. They sent me to Frankfurt, Germany, instead, where I worked in the clinic and often served as a midwife. I loved seeing the babies being born. I also did a lot of immunizations on base—vaccinating everyone from infants to adults. People often had not been immunized in quite a while, so they required multiple doses. Small children sometimes needed four to five injections. By the time I finished this mission, I was experiencing such homesickness.

Part of my work in Germany involved working in the psych unit on base. It was my introduction to seeing combat stress first-hand. Soldiers came in experiencing symptoms such as headaches, back pains, shaking and tremors, nausea and vomiting, heart palpitations, and nightmares, but they often couldn't pinpoint what had happened to cause the symptoms. When they did talk, they talked about being under constant tension and threat from bullets, land mines, and explosives, about the difficulty of seeing dead people and those who had been severely wounded. They were often exhausted and had difficulty processing the simplest of tasks. There was a great nurse there who headed up the psych ward. She had been a nurse in Vietnam and was black and loud and called things as she saw them. Nobody ever talked about combat stress back in Vietnam, she said. It wasn't allowed. But it was real, as real as it is today.

The first Persian Gulf War was short, just six months officially. Our unit was back to the States before long. I was a little upset that I didn't get a chance to go to Kuwait at that time. It's hard to explain it fully. Now that I was in the military, I wanted to experience it all. If I was an army nurse, then I wanted to be as close to the action as I could. In honesty, I don't know if the possibility of excitement drew me, or the prospect of helping wounded troops. But I was an army nurse through and through, and I felt disappointment at not being near the combat zone.

Our family went through some transitions in those years while I was going on all those missions with the reserves. In late fall 1991, my dear father went in for bypass surgery. Septicemia set in, and his whole body was inflamed with infection. For nine weeks, he lingered in the hospital's intensive care unit. He was medicated and couldn't talk, but he was alert. His eyes would watch me whenever I came into the room. I came every day. My mother's birthday is Christmas Eve, and I know he didn't want to die on her birthday. Her birthday passed and I went to see him. "Daddy, you can go now," I said. "We'll take good care of Mommy for you." He held on for five more days, then died just before New Year's Eve. My mother was devastated. She and Daddy were opposites, but they always connected. They had enjoyed a wonderful marriage. She had lost her best friend. I had lost a man I loved and looked up to enormously, and I would never stop missing him.

More missions followed for me. I didn't let up. In 1994, I was back in the States. George had a new job with the Providence Water Supply Board. I was a major by then and received an urgent call. "Major Luz, we need you as an interpreter in Guatemala. You speak Spanish. Be prepared to leave in two days."

"Two days?" I said. "I've got a hair appointment at the end of the week. Do you know how hard it is to schedule a good hair appointment?"

"You're packing your bags. You're going. Two days."

I went, wisps of gray hair and all. It was a higher-risk mission than I'd been on previously. We gathered at the hangar at Hanscom Air Force Base in preparation for leaving. There was a TV on in the hangar, and *60 Minutes* came on with a piece about an American woman who had been killed recently by the Guatemalan Indians because they thought she had come to steal babies. We went anyway, but those images never completely left our minds. Our mission involved setting up medical outposts. I helped at the clinics and interpreted when needed. While I was gone, I was set to receive the Feinstein Foundation's Teacher of the Year Award. George and my mother went and received the award for me. While I was on base, some reporter from the United States came and wanted to do a story about me—the Providence teacher of the year serving her country overseas. The guy wanted to photograph me indoors, but I said, "No way, we've got to go outside where I can wear a hat." I didn't want them seeing my gray hair.

It was sort of a strange mission all around. On the way down to Guatemala, I was sitting next to Major Deniece Barnett-Scott, a new officer attached to our unit. She was a short black woman with beautiful white teeth. Everyone thought she was real highbrow because she didn't talk to anybody. I thought she spent all this money on teeth whitener, but after I got talking to her for a while, she warmed up to me and told me it was just baking soda. We had a good laugh about it, shaking in our seat belts, and I knew the barriers were down. When we landed, we took a bus to the base. The ride was hellish, the driver the devil. On a particularly tight hairpin turn, the driver passed another car on the opposite side of the road. Major Barnett-Scott walked up to him and snapped a picture with her camera. She came back to where I was sitting. "Major Luz, when they find my dead body here, you show them this picture if you survive. Tell my husband about this driver. He's a lawyer and he's gonna sue their ass." From that point onward all we did was laugh.

Another woman in our unit on that mission was acting strangely. She was constantly criticizing people, telling us we were weirdos. She doused her bed with moth flakes, convinced they were going to ward off any evil spirits that might be in the area. It was rainy season in Guatemala, and the moth flakes mixed with the moisture and rose in the air. I had an allergic reaction to the flakes and lost my voice for three days. Major Barnett-Scott took the woman aside and told her to look sharp and cut out the crap with the moth flakes. Without a doubt I knew the major was a permanent ally.

IN 1997, MY SISTER, Ellen-Ann, and her daughter, Katie, went to visit our mother one day and found that they couldn't get in the front door. Mom always bolted the door, but we all had keys. Ellen-Ann called me. By the time I arrived, the fire department was already there. They had broken down the door and found my mother on the floor, the phone off the hook nearby. She had suffered a massive stroke but was still breathing. They rushed her to the hospital. My mother's father had been bedridden for seven years before he passed. My mother had cared for him during that time; afterward, she always said that when her time was up she wanted to go quickly. She got her wish. She was only 78 when she died. We all miss her terribly. Not a day goes by in which I don't think of my mother. Of all the people in my life, she influenced me most. She was who I aspired to be when I grew up.

In 1998, George's dad died in a horrible accident. He worked on large industrial dryers. One of the dryers, about 7,200 pounds, slipped off its supports and fell on him. Doctors said he died instantly. So many people in the area knew and loved George Luz Sr. A line of people stretched out the door of the funeral parlor and around the block; 1,600 people came to pay their respects. There was not enough room for everybody.

ALSO IN 1998, I ACHIEVED the rank of lieutenant colonel. My unit went to Kosovo in 2000, but I didn't go. It was a six-month, all-volunteer mission, and I didn't want to be away from George that long. Plus, I would have needed to do medical-surgical work over there, and I had never enjoyed that. When he was still alive, my father, though always the army man, had encouraged me not to step forward if I didn't have to.

One of the main reasons I didn't want to go to Kosovo, however, was that my nephew, Geoffrey, was having his first lung transplant, and I wanted to be around for the family. He was 17 when he received the first transplant, a senior in high school. We had gone to Disney World as a family right before. Geoffrey had been very weak, and we pushed him around in a wheelchair. He loved Disney World. "If I'm going to go," he said, "this is a great place to be if it happens."

A friend of his with CF was ahead of him in line to receive a new set of lungs. A call came, and she went in for the procedure. She was prepped and already on the operating table at Children's Hospital Boston, but at the last minute she changed her mind. We don't know why. The lungs went to Geoffrey instead.

Let me depart from my narrative for a moment and continue this story up to the present: Geoffrey's first transplant lasted a good four years and saw him almost all the way through college. But toward the end of his senior year, he started to feel unwell again. He survived his second transplant—the one he had in March 2006, right before I left for Iraq—and thrived for a while, but the success didn't last long. He soon needed another transplant, his third. Triple lung transplants are virtually unheard of. A whole consortium of doctors weighed in on the odds. Finally, the Cleveland Clinic agreed to do the procedure. In 2008, my nephew, Geoffrey Higginbotham, became the first American to have three lung transplants, thanks to the Cleveland Clinic, and, of course, thanks to the anonymous donor. This third transplant will buy my nephew some more time. I know in my heart that three is a charm, and number three is going to last forever.

My other two nephews with CF, Matthew and Ryan, have never had transplants. They've both been in the hospital quite a bit and have endured lives of coughing, but fortunately they haven't been sick enough to need transplants. We keep hoping that someday there will be a cure for cystic fibrosis.

MY LIFE NEVER STOPPED for long, even for family concerns. In 2001, I went to Germany again on another mission. We flew home on September 9, just two days before the tragic events of September 11. The HBO miniseries *Band of Brothers* had premiered in Normandy a few months before. We held a private premiere in Rhode Island as well, with limos and a lot of food in a fancy hotel. When the series premiered on HBO on September 9, it drew ten million viewers. Then, when the attacks of September 11 occurred, HBO immediately ceased its marketing campaign. The second episode nonetheless drew some seven million viewers. I think we as a nation were hungry for heroes. We wanted to make sense of both our history and our present.

When the second war in the Persian Gulf was declared in 2003, my reserve unit was activated almost immediately, but my own involvement was delayed. The thinking was that combat stress nurses are usually more needed as a war progresses. I was called up for an assignment to Iraq in 2004, but the mission eventually went to another nurse. They wanted to send nurses in twos, as part of the partner system, and since this other woman's nursing partner was already signed up, the two of them had priority.

In 2004, I became a full-bird colonel and went to Bolivia on another humanitarian mission. The entire mission was a wild ride. The area was rife with civil unrest, with violent protests a common occurrence. We were not allowed to go beyond the walls of our station, except on official duty. Again, our job was to set up small clinics in rural areas. The days were long, beginning at five each morning and continuing late into the night. Conditions were primitive on the Bolivian base: dirt everywhere, no showers, no hot water. None of us carried weapons on this mission, since we were not in an official war zone, but we had armed Special Forces with us at all times. We were set to be there 21 days, but were delayed 7 days in coming home, so I was there more than a month. Some 80 people were killed at the airport right after we left. I was so glad to get out of the country.

In some ways, the years after 2001 blur together in my mind as a stream of different kinds of wars, all of which needed a nightingale's song, but not a sentimental song. I conditioned myself to serve, not to focus on feeling. So much of the need I saw seemed beyond emotion. My response was not to shed tears, but to roll up my sleeves. That became my mode of operation. It was a mode that would serve me well in the next chapter of my life.

Then it came.

My hands shook slightly when the letter arrived from the Department of the Army, March 30, 2006. The letter announced that my reserve unit had been officially activated for mobilization in support of Operation Iraqi Freedom, and I would soon be deployed to Iraq for up to 545 days.

That was the letter I had been waiting for my whole life. I welcomed it, yet I dreaded it, too. When you've been a nurse for as long as I have, you prepare yourself for these things. I reminded myself that any type of service, if it's worth doing, usually involves some kind of difficulty, some kind of pain. In my honest moments, I feared the worst.

❖

PART THREE

The Nightingale Sings

CHAPTER 11

In a War Zone

OCTOBER 2006, MOSUL, IRAQ: Even at dawn I could hear
traffic—car horns and accelerating engines and the throaty
rumble of diesel buses—from where I lay in my bunk inside my
contained housing unit (CHU) on the military base at Camp
Diamondback. There was already a lot of activity going on outside the base, even this early in the morning. I could hear sporadic
small-arms fire, too, little booms echoing off the horizon, and I
didn't know if the noise was simply a local disturbance or if we
were about to become busy again in the hospital within the next
20 minutes. I took a shower anyway, changed clothes, and put
on a bit of makeup, then headed over to the mess tent to grab
a bite of breakfast. The traffic and the sporadic small-arms fire
continued to mingle. I didn't know it then, but that would become
the regular soundtrack of our time in Mosul.

After breakfast, we pinned a Purple Heart and a Combat
Action Badge on PFC Tara Edminston, the young woman who
had taken shrapnel in the stomach during yesterday evening's
mortar attacks. Her eyes fluttered open as she lay in the intensive
care unit. Her close friend Major Heidi Kelly was the first person
she saw. This morning marked PFC Edminston's 52nd week in
Iraq. The first 51 weeks had gone safely for her, and she should

have been looking forward to going home. Instead, after the small bedside ceremony, they loaded her into a helicopter to be flown to a recovery hospital in Germany.

Next, an official change-of-command ceremony was held. Members of the unit we were replacing grabbed their gear, ran out onto the airstrip, and boarded the planes headed back to Kuwait and then to the United States. We were alone now, officially on our own. I sensed a renewed resolve throughout our unit. All of us had come a long way to get to this place in our lives. The bulk of the real work was just beginning.

Soon we held a briefing with Major General Ronald D. Silverman, who was in charge of all health care in Iraq. He gave us a bird's-eye perspective on our mission. Iraq, he said, is a country of about 168,000 square miles, about the same size as California. That's a lot of territory to be covered; a lot is going on at any one time. Our military medical system in Iraq, he noted, offers 250 beds throughout the whole country; by comparison, each major hospital back in the States has about 1,000 beds at its disposal. Yet despite our small size, we were considered the world's largest trauma center. We needed to be relentlessly efficient, consistently adept at doing our jobs. We were the frontline care system in a combat zone.

Major General Silverman reminded us that whatever resources we needed to keep U.S. troops healthy, or to help them get healthy, would be available to us. For instance, a soldier had recently been burned badly. He bypassed the hospital in Germany and was flown immediately from Iraq to the military's foremost burn center at Fort Sam Houston, Texas. The plane he was on needed to be refueled several times midflight, but the army got him there in time to save his life and significantly aid his recovery.

I soon came to understand that our health care system in

Iraq worked as follows: Typically, wounded soldiers and civilians went from battle zones to military emergency rooms, one of which was the 399th, where immediate lifesaving procedures were performed. Then within 48 hours maximum, the wounded left Iraq and were flown to Landstuhl Regional Medical Center, the American overseas hospital in Germany, where more definitive care could be given, and from there back to the States or back to their units. In addition to emergency procedures, the 399th was also tasked with offering routine medical care for soldiers and military contractors stationed in Iraq. Cold medications, flu shots—whatever treatment was needed to get or keep people healthy, that was our job to provide.

Major General Silverman warned us that although we were skilled medical professionals, we would see injuries in Iraq that we had never before seen in the States. Back in Providence, a surgeon might see a gunshot wound, a burn, or a leg broken in three places—but the surgeon wouldn't generally see all those injuries in the same patient at the same time. In Iraq, we would regularly see patients with multiple traumas. This would often require multiple surgical teams to work on each patient, something not commonly done in the States.

Following that introduction, we got to work. My immediate boss, Colonel Joseph Blansfield, along with my DCC, Colonel Joaquin Cortiella, ran the 399th hospital. He gave me great freedom to implement my job. "Go out to the other units on base and introduce yourself," Colonel Blansfield said. So I did. There were at least 25 units on base, maybe more: Special Forces, engineers, civilian contractors, postal units, infantry units—it takes a lot of people to run an overseas military base during wartime.

So over the next few days, I went out to the other units and said over and over, "Hi, I'm Colonel Luz, the new public health nurse in town. Come see me if you need this, this, or this." The idea was to spread the word that all military personnel needed to stay healthy. I met a lot of people and made a lot of good connections.

My job also involved inspecting the dining hall, making sure people stored food properly and used gloves when handling it. I went out with the veterinarian on base whenever he gave shots to animals, and I talked about rabies. I didn't have my own vehicle, but the vet had a Humvee, so I often rode with him to visit the units—that, or I walked. I could get a lot of places within Diamondback on foot, but to get over to the adjoining Camp Marez was too far. Anytime I walked anywhere, the desert sand stuck to me. I used to think "desert" and imagine *Lawrence of Arabia,* the old British movie starring Peter O'Toole, with its picturesque backdrops and gently rolling sand dunes. But the sand in Iraq, at least where we were stationed, is more like brown talcum powder. It's desiccated dirt, like fine dust. Whenever the wind picked up, which was most afternoons, the sandy dust blew everywhere in huge tan clouds. A brown film of powder soon covered everything. Inside my CHU, I covered my gear with plastic. It didn't matter. Dust was everywhere. A rainy season would come in a few months. I imagined the dust turning to a thick, ankle-deep muck. I hoped that would be the only trouble that awaited us. Somehow, though, I knew it wouldn't be.

THE MORTARS KEPT COMING. Shells blasted our compound regularly. They became part of a savage routine. The loudspeakers bristled, the announcement sounded, we sprinted to bunkers, a report of all clear followed, and then we treated whoever was wounded. For many in our unit, the training simply set in. You remain calm, get low, and wait for the all clear. Then you double-time it over to the hospital, hugging the blast walls all the way.

I believe those first few weeks were the hardest time for many in our unit yet also, strangely, the best. They were the best because there was no second-guessing our mission; we sensed anew that we were truly there and truly needed. They were the worst because you can't prepare, you can't actually grasp what it's like to be in a war zone. Every sunup brings a new day of someone wishing you were dead.

One afternoon around two, a mortar came in and hit one of the CHUs but didn't go off. We saw right away that we'd been extremely fortunate it had been a dud, because it could have taken out the whole street. When the mortar came in, it flew straight through the open window of the CHU and ripped a medical shirt (scrub top) hanging on a chair. The next day, the sergeant who lived in the CHU wore that same ripped scrub on his rounds as a statement of defiance to fate. A few days later, the sergeant was heading to the mess hall for dinner when another mortar flew right by him, landed in a tree, but also didn't go off. It would have killed him for sure. "Must have been an angel sitting on my shoulder," he said wryly. I noted that after the second incident he didn't wear his ripped scrub top anymore. He didn't want to mess with the cosmos, I guess.

As the weeks passed, I slowly adjusted to the craziness of the situation. Almost each new day, we received wounded coming off the field. About half our casualties came to us by ground—they had been wounded in Mosul or nearby areas and came to us by ambulance or Humvee. Almost by pattern, troops went out on patrol, got into trouble and sustained casualties, then turned around and drove back right up to the front door of the 399th. The other half of our patients came to us by helicopter. They had been fighting in other parts of the country, and if we were the closest hospital, they came to us. We rapidly learned how to unload and extract the wounded from a variety of army vehicles, many of which we had never seen up close before. Many patrols were done in armored five-ton trucks with turrets that looked like something out of the movie *Mad Max*. We also received wounded in a variety of American SUVs and pickups that were strangely modified by civilian contractors. They came to us in tractor-trailer trucks, in tanks, in huge CH-47 Chinooks (the twin-rotor helicopters that look like flying scorpions), and in UH-60 Blackhawks (the more regular-looking four-bladed helicopters).

Most of our patients were Americans. We also received coalition troops, Iraqi soldiers and policemen, civilians caught in cross fire, insurgent prisoners of war, and children. The children were always the hardest. Kids would be out playing on the street, walking to school, running errands to the store—just doing normal kid things—and they'd get hit from mortar blasts or improvised explosive devices (IEDs). We saw loss of limbs, chunks of shrapnel sticking out of little bodies. Some children's limbs were amputated in the blasts. One day a child fell off a wall after a blast occurred and was brought to us with head trauma; he lived. Another day a child came who had been hit in the head with a bullet; he died. (Iraqis often shot their rifles into the air—to celebrate, to vent frustration, because a soccer team scored a goal—the reasons seemed unending. Well, those bullets had to come down somewhere.)

One day insurgents bombed a school. They were mad at something and decided to take it out on their community. We received five elementary-aged children that day. Their eyes were round with fear. They were wounded to begin with, and many of them were not used to being around Americans. A lot of good activity went into taking care of the wounded kids. It seemed that all the nurses and medical personnel wanted to be around them. We brought them little toys and gifts, candy if they were able to eat it. There was so much activity around the kids that the officer in charge (OIC) of our intermediate care ward (basically the head nurse), Lieutenant Colonel Gloria Vignone, needed to good-naturedly curtail it.

I thought the world of Lieutenant Colonel Vignone. We both affectionately referred to each other as "the Old Hag." I developed a reputation fairly early on of being a person who could get things. Somehow I had commandeered a love seat and had set it up in my office. The Old Hag saw it, flopped down on it, and ran her hand along its soft cushions. "Wow, where'd you get this bit of heaven?" she said. The next day I commandeered one for her office as well.

The children weren't all innocent. One 16-year-old boy came to us as a prisoner of war. He had been shooting at coalition troops, or perhaps planting IEDs, doing something to get arrested anyway. He was healthy enough to want to check his email, but we didn't let him. Even at his young age he was considered a potential security threat—a sad but true reality of the war.

As a senior officer, I was sometimes made aware that we could likely expect an influx of wounded. The war fighters in our area notified our tactical operations center (TOC), and the TOC notified us in turn that an operation was beginning. For instance, a particular neighborhood in Mosul might be identified by army intelligence as having a lot of insurgent activity. So the infantry would make a coordinated search. The key intersections around a neighborhood would be closed off so that no traffic could flow in or out, then our troops would make a building-by-building sweep of the area. They often found caches of weapons, explosives, and combat supplies, or encountered the insurgents themselves. That's when injuries were likely. Beforehand, we would receive enough information to know the approximate time an operation was to take place, a general idea of where, and an approximate idea of the mission's nature. When we had this information, we were able to be better prepared. We made sure that our blood bank was topped up, our equipment was ready, and our duty rosters were double-checked. When information came, key leadership personnel walked around the hospital a bit more deliberately. Sometimes nothing came of it, but usually there were several casualties.

More frequently, the wounded came to us with no briefing beforehand. This happened whenever troops were out on patrol and drew sniper fire or encountered an IED, a suicide bomber, or the like. We'd just take these as they came. A normal daily load for us would be to receive two to six wounded at a time.

One morning around 11:00, Colonel Blansfield was notified that a suicide car bombing had occurred in Tal Afar, a city about 15 miles due west from us by air. There were 22 confirmed dead and 30 wounded. We would be getting 16 surgical immediates by helicopter, 4 per chopper, and the first would arrive in about ten minutes. A shiver went down my spine. The MASCAL code immediately went out over the loudspeakers. Through my mind flashed a picture of our hospital's six trauma bays, three operating-room (OR) tables, and 12 intensive care unit (ICU) beds. Half of the ICU beds were already occupied. Now we were getting 16 new wounded all at once. We simply didn't have the resources to handle them.

As the first chopper landed, our teams raced over to receive the wounded, and triage became very sophisticated. The danger in an operation like this comes when you immediately take whoever comes first and send him directly into the operating room. Your first patient might have a minor wound to one of his extremities, and then on the next chopper you might find a patient with a gaping chest wound who needs surgery right away. You might also find that a patient is beyond your capability. For instance, we had no neurosurgery capability at the 399th, so any patients with bleeding in the brain were evacuated to Baghdad. The solution in a large-scale MASCAL like this was to wait until all 16 patients had landed and were in the triage tent together, and then to take the most seriously wounded first.

The triage unit was soon a beehive of activity. There was a lot of gore. Several of the wounded were missing limbs. Several others had open belly wounds. Our team was packing and clamping right and left so that the wounded wouldn't bleed to death. Blood soaked the concrete floor already. Blansfield sent several of the wounded who required minor operations to the ICU to be treated because there were more open tables there.

We found out later that the carnage had come as the result of a perfect storm of insurgency. A suicide bomber had driven his vehicle into an area of the city where a car auction was taking place. He had offered his vehicle for sale at a low price. Once he had gathered a large crowd around his vehicle, he backed away and detonated the bomb in his car. When responders came to render aid and put out the fire, the insurgent ran back to the crowd, unnoticed in the commotion, and detonated the explosives strapped to his body—a deadly and tragic double strike.

Perhaps the strangest part of the situation happened when one of the wounded, a man with a gaping coffee-cup-sized wound to the groin area, was taken through our CAT scan machine. The images showed a dense white object in the man's lower abdomen that should not have been there. The surgeons retraced the wound and discovered that it was actually a rib fragment. The strangest part? The rib didn't come from the wounded man. The rib cage of the suicide bomber had been blasted with such force that a piece of rib had propelled itself into this other man. The bomber's own ribs became weapons.

The army color-codes triage categories in ascending order. Green means "minimals," yellow means "delays," red means "immediates," and black means "expectants" (those expected to die). The last category came to me. One of the expectants that day had a crushed skull. He was also missing a limb. The man was heavily sedated but still breathing. His breaths came out raspy and labored. I dabbed his lips with cool water, checked his vitals, and held his hand until he passed. It wasn't long, maybe half an hour. For all patients brought to me, my goal was to do whatever I could to make them comfortable. If they were on my watch, everybody was going to be looked after well, even if there was no chance at saving them.

That day everybody worked at least a 12-hour shift in addition to their regular duties before and after the MASCAL. The tempo continued inside the hospital as the 16 wounded were transferred from the ER to the OR and then to the ICU.

That night I lay in my bunk, again physically exhausted but mentally wide awake. I replayed the scenes I had just witnessed over and over in my mind. My familiar outrage burned within me at the atrocities of war. I tossed and turned, again unable to sleep.

IN NOVEMBER, MY HEART gave a little leap when I heard that a new unit was coming to base, the 4th Brigade Combat Team, 1st Cavalry Division, from Fort Bliss, Texas. They were essentially an infantry unit, tasked with the dangerous mission of going out into the city of Mosul each day to look for bad guys and keep things calm.

What made my heart leap was that this was Second Lieutenant Chris Manion's unit. As I mentioned earlier, Chris was the son of Donna, my lifelong friend from college and the Peace Corps. Before I came to Iraq, Donna had said that Chris's unit was heading over, but as is standard procedure, she wasn't told exactly when or where. The specifics of a unit's whereabouts are seldom made public. Having young Chris Manion over here would feel like having a big piece of family from home.

Chris grew up in a Massachusetts town just across the border from Rhode Island, close enough for me to function in an active role in his life for many years. He was born in January 1983, just before my nephews Geoffrey and John Patrick. I was there in the labor room with Donna when she gave birth. Chris came out as a feisty redhead, always on the go. He became like a son to me. There were all the childhood years of birthday presents, toys, GI Joes, and such. He was an only child and we heaped the gifts on him. I came for many celebrations. Chris went to an all-boys' Catholic school. He excelled in golf and loved to work out with weights. He never stood still for long. To celebrate his high school graduation, we all went on a Caribbean cruise together: Joe, Donna, and Chris Manion; our good friends Elaine and John D'Antuono; and George and I. Chris went to college and graduated from the University of Maryland, then enlisted in the army. He had a girlfriend back home, a cute, blue-eyed pharmacy student in Austin, Texas, where Chris's unit was stationed. He loved being a soldier, and he also loved her. There were rumors of a ring soon.

I knew the date when Chris's unit was coming in, but I didn't know the specific plane. A unit arrives in several planes, and specific information isn't announced. Heading over to the airstrip near the base just after supper, I planned to stay and wait until Chris arrived. Planes began to land. The planes zigged and zagged on their way down to avoid sniper fire, same as when our unit landed. Then, once the planes were stationary on the tarmac, soldiers sprinted to the bunkers, then headed into the terminal area to have their IDs rechecked to get on base. An hour passed. Then another. Planes kept arriving. The terminal was soon filled with a steady influx of men in flak jackets and camouflage pants and helmets, all carrying duffel bags and rifles. Still no Chris.

The last plane of the night landed. It was nine o'clock, almost dark. The desert wind blew dusty and cool through the late-evening sky, uncharacteristically cold for Mosul. I was wearing a black fleece jacket and a tam, like a little tote hat, that covered my ears. My rank wasn't visible. Suddenly, I spotted Chris's tall frame, his bulky shoulders and blue eyes. He was one of the last off the last plane. I ran to him and gave him a big hug and kiss.

"Hey, my mom's going to be happy now!" Chris said, and hugged me back. We were both grinning.

"Man, just look at this place," said the kid next to Chris in line. "What a goddamn hellhole this is."

"Uh, dude, this is *Colonel* Luz," said Chris to the kid, subtlely letting him know that his language wasn't appropriate around a senior officer.

"Ma'am, I'm sorry, ma'am," the kid said.

I guess the kid wasn't used to colonels running up and hugging Second Lieutenant Chris Manion. I told the kid not to worry about it. This wasn't a time for formalities.

Chris turned to the kid and grinned. He introduced me all around. "She's like my second mother," Chris said to all the guys.

I brought Chris a few gifts to make him feel at home: a cell phone, a tiny microwave, and a coffee pot for his CHU. That evening I walked with him as far as I could, then we promised we'd see each other soon. I went back to my office and called Donna in the States. We had talked several times already since

I had been in Iraq. She can be a bit of a worrier, always expecting the worst, but then again, it's normal to worry if those you love are in Iraq. She knew about George's cousin Brian St. Germain, the young soldier killed in the flash flood.

"Donna," I said. "Chris is here. He's with me."

That's all I needed to say. Donna started crying. You have to be careful what you say on the phone from a combat military base. I couldn't disclose our exact location. But Donna knew enough. She was so glad.

Chris was stationed fairly close to me in the Camp Marez portion of the base. He was a smart kid. At the start, he was an executive officer (XO) of his company, which meant he was with headquarters planning out the missions. But as time went on, he started feeling upset that he wasn't going out on missions with the men. He wanted to do his part outside the base's walls. So he approached his company commander, volunteered to leave headquarters, and became a platoon leader. I never told Donna this. Chris made me promise I wouldn't.

November 2006 also marked the end of Saddam Hussein's trial. The former dictator was found guilty of crimes against humanity. In Baghdad's Green Zone, a five-judge Iraqi panel announced a unanimous sentence of death for Saddam and two of his seven co-defendants, including Saddam's half brother. The news drew mixed results throughout Iraq. Some danced in the streets, celebrating. Others strapped explosives on themselves and vowed revenge.

Mosul, along with several major cities, was under a strict curfew prior to the Saddam verdict. When the verdict came, there were a few demonstrations—both pro and con—but thankfully no major spikes in insurgent activity. We took three mortar strikes on the base. It was mostly shoot-and-scoot stuff, a calm day. Insurgents fired at us from the backs of pickup trucks from different parts of the city and then zipped away. By the time our fighters responded, the insurgents were long gone and our aerial drones couldn't pick them up fast enough. Fortunately, the insurgents were bad shots.

I went over to see Chris quite a bit. I brought goody bags for him and his buddies, stuff people had sent from the States mostly, cookies, candy, socks, T-shirts. One day we received 200 boxes of Girl Scout cookies, and I took them all over for the guys. Near the holidays, I was able to commandeer a Christmas tree—artificial, but still complete with decorations—and took that over. I brought presents for everybody and developed a bit of a bond with the unit.

I got to know two other kids from Chris's unit. The first was Sergeant Brent Dunkleberger. I call him a kid, but really he wasn't. He was a bit older than Chris, maybe in his late 20s, from Bloomington, Pennsylvania, married, with four young children. Sergeant Dunkleberger had worked as a firefighter before joining the military. He had reddish hair just like Chris's, and a clear, broad smile. He was always joking. I liked him immediately. Once for a New Year's parade back home, he dressed up like a big New Year's baby and walked the parade route complete with diaper and baby bottle. This was his second tour of duty in Iraq. He reminded me of Chris quite a bit. From a distance, I sometimes even confused the two.

The second was Specialist Matthew T. Grimm. He was shorter than Sergeant Dunkleberger, stockier, and younger, maybe 19 or 20, and had an unforgettable smile. He came from Wisconsin and had graduated from high school as a star football player, wrestler, and weight lifter. He joined the military right out of high school. Specialist Grimm loved stock cars and had been a part of his cousin's racing team. He had a life of adventure and service ahead of him. I took to him immediately.

Second Lieutenant Chris Manion. Sergeant Brent Dunkle-berger. Specialist Matthew T. Grimm. They were just three among many, faces in a crowd of soldiers, strong and bright young men with promising futures. Each could look forward to so much life ahead.

I continued thinking about them when the weather cooled off and we started to get our first real winter rains. The rains came in bursts, like liquid bullets on our helmets. There were no storm drains or gutters anywhere, so water pooled when it rained and flooded the roads and low areas. As I'd expected, the desert dust quickly turned to a thick brown muck. Furrows developed in the compound, marshy trenches of war. Every so often, a big suck-truck came around and vacuumed everything, and the muck wasn't much higher than our boots then. The foul weather caused us to bear down more, to bite our lips, to fight the foreshadowing darkness that inevitability greeted each new day.

IT WAS DECEMBER 11, 2006, early in the evening. I remember the date because I was thinking it was only two weeks until Christmas—not that there was much holiday shopping to do in Iraq. There were shops on base and smaller Iraqi-run shops near the compound where you could get fake Rolex watches and pirated DVDs, but I wasn't thinking much about shopping just now anyway. This year my old thoughts about the Massacre of the Innocents returned: Jesus was born and baby boys died. Christmas and death. How many years had it been? Donna and I had just walked out into the hot Brazilian sun after taking communion in Quixadá, and the fog in my spirit was drifting away. I had long since learned that if the world was actually all that nice, as I had once imagined, then Christ would not have needed to come to it in the first place. So to truly follow in the footsteps of Christ's mission, like I was trying to do, I also needed to understand and face the reality of horror. I hoped I had experienced all I would ever need to in that category.

That day, December 11, flu season was coming on, and I had just returned to the hospital from being out on the base giving flu shots. Usually, I would head back to my CHU about seven, but for some reason I lingered in the hospital that evening. I was almost ready to head back when outside there was a sudden blast. We all heard it, even as far inside the walls on base as we were. My first thought was *Car bomb!* Someone yelled, "IED!" Then the call came: "Incoming wounded!"

Chris often wouldn't tell me about his missions. I didn't even know his unit was going out that night. The news of the blast came instantly, although filtered in bits and pieces. His unit had been heading out in a convoy on a security mission when they were struck by a rocket-propelled grenade. "We just got word," Colonel Blansfield said. His face was somber. "No wounded. Just dead. They'll head straight to the morgue."

The Humvees that were still running in Chris's unit rushed back through our gates, but for some reason they came straight up to the hospital instead of the morgue. Maybe there were survivors after all. For several minutes all was noise and chaos. A squad of soldiers jumped out of the Humvee, lifted a soldier, and carried him in. Doctors and surgical nurses swarmed around the man. I couldn't get close to see what was happening. One soldier, a particularly stocky man with his rifle slung in position, looked close to tears, a mixture of anger and grief. "My God!" he said. "Why did this have to happen? Why?"

That's when I glimpsed red hair.

It was limp and matted and caked with blood and sticking out from the sides of the helmet on the soldier being carried in by his buddies. The red hair was unmistakable. "Chris. Chris," I whispered. "Please, God—no! How am I ever going to tell Donna?"

There was a soft tap on my shoulder. "Colonel Luz?" It was Specialist Elizabeth Tice, the sweetheart of a girl who handled preventive medicine and often worked with me. She was shaking her head, as if sensing what I was feeling. "That's not Second Lieutenant Manion," she said. "Look at the name badge."

Three things occurred virtually simultaneously. My eyes darted from the wounded soldier's red hair to his badge, and instantly I felt enormous relief. It plunged over me as if I were standing underneath a waterfall. Second, a doctor pronounced the wounded soldier dead on arrival. This meant I would be responsible for the body until the coroner came. Then, mixed with the relief, I also felt instant, enormous shame. It crept through me and settled darkly into my stomach. This was some other mother's son on the table. Someone's brother. Someone's friend. Here I was, feeling relief at my own good fortune when very shortly another woman, another mother, another father, another brother, another town, another community—so many people—would feel the pain of this loss.

I looked closer at the name badge. I stared at it this time in horror and felt a fourth emotion. This new darkness gripped me and wouldn't let go. Once for a New Year's parade back home, this soldier had dressed up like a big New Year's baby and walked the parade route complete with diaper and baby bottle. This man was so full of life, always joking, with a clear, broad smile. He looked so much like Chris that from a distance, sometimes I even confused the two. This was Sergeant Brent Dunkleberger. My body trembled at the reality of who it was on the table.

"No! This isn't happening!" The words came from the stocky soldier with his rifle slung in position. He pounded the wall with his fist.

I walked over to him, my body still trembling. "He was your friend, yes?"

The stocky soldier nodded.

"He was my friend, too," I murmured.

The stocky soldier collapsed in my arms, sobbing.

He wasn't the only one. Another soldier stood motionless by the door, his hands pressed against his temples as if he were trying to push away the onslaught of an enormous migraine. Another slumped in a chair, a faraway look in his eyes. Still another ran out the door.

When a soldier dies, you're not supposed to wipe the blood off his face. Only the coroner does this. But I felt so sorry for Sergeant Dunkleberger that I didn't want his buddies to remember his face matted with blood. Out of respect for this young man, I asked for a cloth and wiped away what I could. Other soldiers from his unit started coming in to pay their last respects. They trickled in slowly over the next few hours as word spread through the unit. Some of the soldiers had gone on to finish the mission and were now just coming back. Some came in with dirt and blood all over them. After Sergeant Dunkleberger was hit with the rocket, they had held him.

Colonel Blansfield had been mistaken from the report he had received: a soldier did come in wounded; he'd been in the same vehicle as Sergeant Dunkleberger. Though he was being carried in on a stretcher, he wanted to touch the body out of respect before he went in for surgery on his arm. "We'll never forget you," he said softly. Then they wheeled him away.

Specialist Matthew T. Grimm was one of the soldiers who

came to say good-bye. He looked at the body of his friend on the cot and his face went white.

I have re-created some of the dialogue for this book to facilitate flow, but this line is exact: "That's going to be me," Specialist Grimm said as if he were having a premonition.

"No, no it's not," I said and laid my hand on his shoulder.

"Yeah, it is," he said. "I just know it."

"It's almost Christmas," I said. "You'll be going home soon."

"No," he insisted. "That's going to be me."

I stuck by the body of Sergeant Brent Dunkleberger for several hours. Early the next morning, they took him away. They would hold an investigation, then put him in a casket and hold a memorial service. His boots would be onstage in memoriam with his rifle and his helmet. Then he would be loaded in the back of a C-130 and flown back to America.

A MONTH LATER, January 15, 2007, Chris Manion's unit was on patrol again when an IED detonated near the vehicle that was traveling ahead of Chris's. The blast made a huge crater in the middle of the road. Four soldiers were killed. Then, stalled on the road trying to deal with the carnage, the survivors took sniper fire. One of the MPs who had come over to help was also shot.

Among the dead on that mission was Specialist Matthew T. Grimm.

Whether he actually received a premonition of his own death the night Sergeant Dunkleberger died, no one will ever know. What I do know is that Matthew T. Grimm was my friend, and I am honored to have served alongside this young man as briefly as I did. I know also that afterward, the rain came down in torrents. It mixed with the dirt and blood and concrete and made a thick, evil slime all over the compound. Everywhere I looked was dark. Every night I could hear the rain pound on my CHU. My eyes remained open. There was no sleeping now.

CHAPTER 12

The Start of the Bloodiest Year

I SQUINTED THROUGH THE window of my CHU into the early-morning Mosul sunlight. It was late December 2006, winter in Iraq. Instead of seeing brown dust and the more recent brown mud, the ground outside was covered in a fine layer of white powder. Snow in Iraq—I couldn't believe it! Memories of home came to me—sleigh rides, fireplaces, Christmas ski trips in upper Vermont.

As I shook myself awake, the happy memories vanished and the ugly rumors I had been hearing lately came back to mind. The scuttlebutt around base was that the war effort wasn't making as much progress as hoped. Stories in the press described the situation in Iraq as spiraling out of control. I walked a fine line between staying up on the news and not listening to it much—on the one hand, I wanted to know what was happening throughout the world; on the other, the news felt too depressing many days. What I could see with my own eyes agreed with many of the news reports, though: violence throughout the city seemed to be growing, not abating. Every few days, we seemed to catch our collective breath and our hospital emptied out. But as soon as it did another wave of wounded filled it up again. You could see the signs of stress begin to show in people. The rub of living in close quarters, the constant pressure of dealing with blood and gore, the stress of being away from home and loved ones—people kept up their professionalism, but tempers flared too quickly. Too often, people snapped in overreaction; lines showed underneath their eyes. We were only a few months into our mission. We still had a long way to go.

The snow was heavy and wet and didn't stay long. Captain Diamond met me at breakfast a few days later, near the start of the New Year.

"Hey, Sue, you hear the news?"

"Nah," I said. "Too busy lately. What's up?"

"They're calling it a troop surge. The president's sending 20,000 more soldiers into Iraq. The idea is that we've got to finish what we started."

"A surge, huh? I hope it works. It would be nice if we saw fewer wounded around here."

"They say it's a controversial plan. But it was recommended by the Iraq Study Group report. More combat troops will get the job done—that's what the report said anyway."

I poured another cup of coffee. "What do you think it'll mean for us?"

Captain Diamond scratched her forehead. "Well, they're saying we've got to protect the Iraqi population somehow until a new government is in place. So I hope more troops make that happen. I dunno—what do you think it'll mean?"

I took a swig and set my cup down. "Things are going to get worse before they get better. That's what this old soldier thinks."

If we could have looked forward a year from that morning near the start of 2007, we'd have seen two things: The good thing was that both critics of the surge and the independent news services alike agreed that the surge did indeed do its job; the visible result on the streets would be a calm unlike any the country had seen since the start of the war. The bad thing was that we paid a heavy price to achieve that calm. My hunch was right: things did get worse before they got better. In a year's time, the Pentagon would look back and declare 2007 the bloodiest year of the war to date. That morning—it was all ahead as something we still needed to live through.

SADDAM HUSSEIN WAS HANGED on December 30, 2006, and all over Mosul people shot their guns into the air, both in celebration and in protest. The biggest barrage of small-arms fire happened about six in the morning our time, and the call quickly came over the loudspeaker for us to don our helmets and body armor. We had previously seen the corollary of similar activity—whatever goes up must come down—and we knew from our firsthand observations that stray bullets can easily kill.

The increased small-arms fire triggered our air defense canopy, and our choppers flew out on patrols. Occasionally, we had practiced an aircraft-in-distress drill. It came in handy a short time later when a helicopter pilot radioed to us, saying he was hit. He landed himself on our medevac pad, and we extricated him directly into the hospital. Random fire had pierced the bottom of his helicopter and hit him in the arm and leg. Fuel and oil were leaking in proximity to live ammo. That's where the drill came in handy, as all the work done near the chopper needed to be done extremely gingerly. I kept my fingers crossed, hoping nothing would explode. Fortunately, the pilot had no life-threatening injuries. He was stabilized, awarded a Purple Heart, and evacuated to Germany in less than four hours.

The days in Mosul became almost routine, if there is such a thing as routine in a war zone. Each day included an early

wake-up, breakfast, wounded people, rounds on base, shots, seminars, dust, lunch, conferences, meetings, more wounded people,
dinner, phone calls, a return to the CHU, bed, and a sleep filled
with tossing and turning. The next day included more of the
same. I held a health fair on base—as big as I could make it. It
felt like a party with fun booths and giveaways and a live band.
People said it came as a welcome respite, but soon afterward the
routine set in again. Then two things happened that broke the
routine. The first was a strong sense within me that something
more needed to be done to boost the morale of our unit, something continuous. We couldn't keep up this pace for long without
all of us going nuts. The second was an order to move.

Our unit was told to prepare to leave Mosul and head for
another base in the western province of Al Anbar. The surge
meant that everything would soon change. The top brass knew
that more soldiers inevitably meant more wounded, and more
wounded meant that more medical care would be needed. Our
new home would be the marine base at Al Asad, located near
Fallujah and Ramadi, two key cities in the war. Most of the
insurgents were located in Al Anbar, and the area was said to
be a hotbed of activity. So that became our new task: to build
a better hospital in a spot where more people were expected to
get shot up.

I should emphasize that we were headed sort of near those
two key cities—ours was to be the nearest military hospital to
them, but the base itself was out in the middle of nowhere. A
seven-mile standoff surrounded the base. Colonel Blansfield came
back from an early trip to scout the area and said he could look
360 degrees in any direction and see nothing but Syrian desert.
In many ways, the isolation meant a greater degree of protection
for us, he noted. Our base in Mosul was in the heart of the city,

right next to the action, but nobody was going to sneak up on us in Al Asad, that was for sure.

It's no small task to move a hospital and all its medical equipment and personnel to a new base. Colonel Blansfield split us into three groups to coordinate the move. Everything we could ship was loaded into huge containers and lifted into C-17 cargo jets by cranes and giant forklifts. Thankfully, none of us needed to travel by ground convoy. The plan was to fly us all to our new home. Just before we were set to leave, an active-duty unit came in to replace us. Their movement into Mosul started the typical surge of mortar attacks that happened whenever a new unit came to base, and for a while mortars rained down on us and exploded all over the base in celebration of the new unit's arrival. Thankfully, there were no casualties this time.

Just prior to the move, I didn't know why I felt such uneasiness in my gut. Then it dawned on me: I actually didn't want to leave Mosul. Leaving Mosul meant leaving Chris Manion and the rest of the guys in his unit. He was a grown young man and could surely take care of himself, but maybe it was the mother's heart in me. If I was around, I thought he would be safer. I talked myself through it. What could I do? Chris was in God's hands. Besides, duty called. My orders were to go. On my last day on base, Chris and I hugged each other and promised we'd try to keep in contact whenever possible.

WE COULD HEAR THE rain beating heavily on the ceiling of the plane as we landed in Al Asad. The rain hit us immediately as we ran down the steps, drenching us as we sprinted to the bunkers. I had seen a lot of rain before in Rhode Island, but this was no ordinary downpour. It soaked us to the skin and saturated our duffel bags and equipment. By the time I found my new quarters, everything felt waterlogged. Everybody sloshed about in the mud. Already among the ranks, there were snarky remarks, grumbling, little tensions. We all hated this new base. We didn't want to be here, wet and cold with the need to become accustomed to everything all over again.

That night my mind went to work as I hung up my wet clothes around the insides of my CHU, hoping they'd dry out in time for me to have something to wear tomorrow. We had a long way to go if we were ever going to be successful in our mission. I felt like grumbling, for sure, but complaining wasn't what I was all about. I thought about what I had seen on the new base, even in this brief time. The CHUs in Mosul had been set up in little streets, but here all the CHUs were set up in one long row. In Mosul, you only got to know the people on your street, but here everyone needed to pass by everyone else to get to their quarters. I filed this observation away in the back of my mind. Something good could come from this new living arrangement. I didn't know exactly what yet, but I knew it could be good. I went to bed, still thinking.

The next morning, the sun came out hot and bright. Little puddles all over the compound evaporated quickly. We didn't know it just then, but that first day's rainstorm was the last moisture we'd ever see in Al Asad. This region was hotter and drier than Mosul. From outside my window, I couldn't see any greenery anywhere. The new base was about 25 square miles, and as far as I could look there were no trees. No flowers. No shrubs. No color except the large green trash containers scattered around the base. Just sand and dust and desert. The wind picked up after breakfast and carried with it a fine layer of gritty powder into the air. All traces of the rainstorm were soon gone, and the air looked like Los Angeles on a bad day. A digital thermometer outside my

CHU read 95 degrees. It wasn't yet nine in the morning. Someone said that our arrival coincided with the start of the dry season. I wondered how hot it would get in the months to come. Digital thermometers were used all over base because regular mercury thermometers only go up to 120 degrees Fahrenheit.

We got to work right away, turning a dilapidated old hospital into a brand-new Level III hospital. There were no Level IIIs anywhere else in Iraq; our hospital in Mosul had been only a Level II. Achieving a new level meant that we would be equipped to handle virtually anything anybody threw at us. It would be a 24-hour military trauma center with in-house coverage by general surgeons and specialists for orthopedic surgery, neurosurgery, anesthesiology, emergency medicine, radiology, internal medicine, oral and maxillofacial surgery, and critical care—basically, everything that is expected in a civilian Level I hospital.

The first day greeted us with the bare insides of new steel modular buildings. That was it: floors, ceilings, walls, electrical power. Nothing more. The rest was up to us. An advance party of contractors had flown in and set up the modulars for us. The plan was to turn the old hospital, a decayed brick building, into our office space. My office would be in the basement of the old building. Across the hall from me was formerly the marines' Angel Room, the room prepared in conjunction with mortuary services to receive the bodies of those who are brought in on Angel Flights. Everyone on duty turns out for Angel Flights. After the choppers land, people stand at attention as the bodies are slowly carried in to the Angel Room. No one looks forward to an Angel Flight, yet no one would miss the ceremony either. I walked into the former Angel Room and looked around, my footsteps echoing. The room felt tomblike and holy. On the walls and floor were flecks of blood. I wondered how many bodies had been laid there to rest. I couldn't imagine ever having regular old meetings in this same room. We couldn't disturb this sacred space.

The next few days were filled with a flurry of activity: ordering supplies, setting up equipment we had brought with us. I roamed the compound in my spare moments, keeping my eyes open to see what I could see. The trash containers looked particularly inviting. They weren't filled with icky garbage, though. At least that's not how I saw them. When the unit before us left, they left in a hurry. There were treasures in these trash bins—desks, chairs, lampshades—a regular goldmine of color and vibrancy for a desert inhabitant with a decorator's eye. Specialist Elizabeth Tice and I often went diving for trash together. We yanked out items that looked interesting and found places for them back in the hospital or the offices. We outfitted many rooms with comfortable tables and chairs, lamps, cabinets. We even found a few Persian rugs. We wanted this place to seem like home as quickly as possible.

IT WAS PROBABLY THE fifth or sixth day in Al Asad. I was pulling a particularly fetching lamp out of the trash, this time by myself, when my heart froze. From the corner of my eye I saw Captain Clint—the commander who had given us so much grief back at Fort McCoy—apparently watching my every move. Her revolver stuck out perpendicular on her hip, same as always, and her hair was pulled back severely in a bun. I had avoided her as much as possible in the past few months in Iraq; people get busy when there's a lot of action going on, and I had mostly succeeded in keeping out of her way. But others still complained about her leadership. Her refrain "And if you don't like the way things are, then too bad" got to be used so much it had morphed from a joke to an old joke to a grating joke—the kind of thing you tense up around whenever you hear it mentioned.

"Colonel Luz," she said. Her voice was strained.

I stopped what I was doing, climbed out of the trash container, and walked over to where she stood. The lamp was still in my hand.

Captain Clint's lips pursed together, opened, then constricted again as if she meant to say something but changed her mind. She swallowed without saying anything. For a few moments we stood looking at each other, neither of us saying a word. Finally, she gave a little nod.

"I'm leaving, you know," Captain Clint said.

"Everything okay?"

"No, not really. They're moving me to another position. Basically, they're getting rid of me, taking me out of leadership—at least that's how it feels."

"I'm sorry to hear that."

"Yeah. Me too."

She swallowed again. I had never seen this side of her. "Can I ask you a question?" she said. "Where did I go wrong? I was just trying to whip this unit into shape, you know—just trying to do my job. Everybody loves you so much. Why did everybody hate me?"

"Nobody hated you," I said. "If you were wounded, everybody would run to take care of you, same as anybody else."

"That's not what I mean. People couldn't stand my leadership. Why? What did I do that was so wrong?"

Now it was I who swallowed. I thought for a minute, searching for something truthful to say, yet kind. I looked at what was in my hand. "I guess I look at my leadership the same way I go looking for things like this lamp," I said. "No one asked me for this lamp, but I figured someone might need it. Maybe it would help somebody feel better here if it was placed on a desk.

It's about listening to people, serving them, helping them out wherever you can."

"I never look at things that way," Captain Clint said. She swiveled and walked away. I wondered if any of my words would take root.

Our new commander was named Captain Tiffany Stockwell. She came in the next day and took charge with a firm, quiet voice. She impressed me immediately as someone straitlaced yet down-to-earth, capable, and kind. You could see that people wanted to do things for her immediately. We were going to be all right with her at the helm.

THERE'S AN OLD SAYING: if you build it, they will come. We finished building and outfitting the new hospital and went through a validation process in which everything was inspected with a fine-tooth comb by our higher command. They examined, documented, and certified everything we had placed our hands on. We passed inspection and held a ribbon-cutting ceremony. It was a really big deal. I counted five army and marine generals and a bunch of other top brass as well as reporters from *Stars and Stripes,* American Forces Network, CNN, and MSNBC. A new group of doctors rotated in to provide more personnel, and new faces mixed with the familiar.

On this new base we had a triage tent outside. (In Mosul, all triage was done inside, as the distance from the chopper pad to the hospital was shorter.) Major General Silverman led us out to the green canvas tent and pointed up to an American flag positioned just below the tent's ceiling. A metal-framed fluorescent light illuminated the flag's red-white-and-blue folds. "You see this?" he said. "This flag marks the golden hour. Anywhere throughout Iraq, if a soldier is wounded on the battlefield, our goal is to get him off the field to a triage tent and into an operating room within 60 minutes or less. We've done the math as it's related to the maps. With the positions of our helicopters, this golden hour is consistently achievable. Right now, whenever a soldier is wounded, if he makes it as far as the triage tent, his chances of surviving are 97 percent. When I talk to troops, I always tell them that if they get to the base hospital and can see the American flag on the ceiling, then they're going to be okay."

Then they came.

On our opening day, we saw our first trauma patient, an insurgent shot by the marines. He was brought to us in handcuffs and guarded the whole time by MPs. All went well and he did fine, an easy day in many ways. On the second day, five civilians were brought to us after their vehicle ran over an IED. Among the wounded was a seven-year-old girl. She had big scared eyes and a bloody bandage around her middle, and she was sobbing in Arabic for her mother—nobody within earshot could fail to recognize that word. All five patients required surgery and were later evacuated.

That evening just before dinner, the thermometer read 119 degrees. As I headed back to my CHU after eating, I had my head down but I noticed the wind picking up. I walked a little quicker. All around me dirt and dust kicked up. Then I looked into the distance, where I could see what I can only describe as a sand tsunami heading in our direction. It looked like a huge brown wave of sky heading straight for the base. For a moment I was awestruck. I actually stopped walking and stared at the thing. The hot wind was really whipping now; it felt like putting a hair dryer to your face. Over the loudspeaker I heard, "Take shelter, get off the roads." I sprinted to my CHU and closed the door just as the sandstorm hit. The sky outside went dark and there was a swishing, swirling sound of sand striking my CHU. The back of my neck bristled. The call came on my pager: "MASCAL! All units report!"

What a horrible time for this to happen—I don't know how the helicopters could have landed in this. I sprinted back in the direction of the hospital's lights, shielding my eyes from the blowing dust with my hand. Along the way, I could just make out a variety of trash containers and portable johns that had been blown over. Not pretty. Another horrible sight greeted us in the hospital: victims from a car bombing were being brought in. I counted the wounded: 9, 10, 11, 12. It was the usual gore—blown-off legs, bloody heads, bandaged eyes, screaming patients—except there were so many this time. All was chaos as the medical-surgical teams ran to help.

Hours later, I don't remember how many, I left the hospital to head back to my CHU. As I walked by an operating room, through the open door I saw an attendant using a large metal wet vac to suck up the blood from the floor. He worked deftly around the surgical table, being careful not to snag the wand on the cords of the anesthesia unit. The operating room housed so much equipment: patient monitors, defibrillators, code carts, EKG units, ventilators, warming cabinets, autoclaves, vaporizers, infusion pumps. Blood puddled all around the bottoms of the carts and cabinets, soaking into the crevices of the tile floor. The attendant's blue-covered boots were speckled with it. There was just so much blood. The image stayed with me and wouldn't leave.

ONE OF MY FIRST large-scale tasks in Al Asad was to organize a series of anthrax immunizations for every person on base, about 20,000 soldiers. It wasn't glamorous work, but it was a military mandate and needed to be done. There are six shots in the anthrax procedure—three to be delivered now in the first series, and three more that could be coordinated after the soldiers rotated back to the States. I went out on base and lined up the units; each day a different unit came to us for the first series. Another nurse, Major Carliss Townes, was in charge of the specialty clinic, and her nurses and medics gave most of the shots. I gave a few, but mostly I coordinated the job. Every once in a while, a big huge soldier passed out. We propped him up and gave him orange juice and cookies. Others resisted the idea of being immunized, but what are you going to do? You'll be given an Article 15 if you refuse an order. I hated to coerce anyone into doing anything he or she didn't want, but this was part of my job. There's just so much unknown about the long-term effects that some younger women on the base were particularly hesitant about getting the shots—they were concerned that the vaccine might affect their ability to get pregnant in the future. I could relate to that fear.

The anthrax series was interspersed with receiving regular wounded. As in Mosul, the wounded typically arrived in groups of two to six, although they seemed to come with more regularity in Al Asad. If was difficult for me to gauge exact numbers, but the surge seemed to be doing what we thought it would. At least we had more advance warning here. In Mosul, about half our wounded came to us by ground vehicle, but in Al Asad, they all came by air. Whenever a call came in, I went to the ER first and got the report, put on my gloves and smock, and headed for the specialty clinic. Major Townes often worked with me. She went to the pharmacy and got morphine. The expectants would arrive. A doctor assessed that they were dead, or nearly, and they came to us for care. Some had IVs still. Once we got an expectant and disagreed with his ranking. We sent him back to the ICU. He lived in the ICU for a while but died in the end.

Day in, day out, the choppers came. There was more blood. More gore. More expectants. More death. The nature of combat is living with highs and lows. One day we might get one or two wounded, then the next we'd get six or eight. When casualties came in, everyone gave 110 percent, but on quieter days, you could see people's exhaustion: the adrenaline had left their bodies and they walked around in a daze. Colonel Blansfield and I met and compared notes.

"We need to keep everyone motivated on a long-term basis," he said. "We've got to keep them going at optimum performance for the duration of our stay here."

"Yeah," I said, "but how?"

"I don't know, Colonel. You're the morale officer."

"Not me," I said. "I've been there, done that. I gave that up long ago."

"Yeah, I know," he said. "But you're the one who's really in charge. You're the unofficial social chairman around here. Everybody knows that. We need your experience. How about another health fair? Tell us all how to stay healthy. Get some new eyeglasses. Get your blood pressure checked. That kind of thing. Make it fun."

"Maybe, but I can't have one of those every week."

"Well, I don't know. Make it a party again. You can organize a party, can't you?"

"Sure, I can organize a party."

"Okay, then." He gave me a little upturned eyebrow, as if there was more he wanted to say. "You're in charge."

I put Colonel Blansfield's suggestion on hold for a while, not quite sure what to do. As a respite from my regular duties, I flew to Camp Liberty in Baghdad. It wasn't a particularly pleasant flight. Flights were often delayed or canceled or rerouted with little notice, and there would be nothing anyone could do. We also now needed to travel with our protective masks and gear due to recent chlorine attacks, as if we didn't already have enough gear to carry around. But that wasn't what made this flight unhappy. I was one of two colonels tasked with escorting a lieutenant colonel to a legal hearing. He had been charged with doing something inappropriate during an ob-gyn exam that he had conducted. I had enough psych training to know that highly unfortunate things like this can sometimes happen when people are under a lot of stress. I wanted to give him the benefit of the doubt, but we didn't talk much during the flight.

Once the lieutenant colonel had been taken where he needed to go, I was free until it was time to fly back. They put me up in one of Saddam Hussein's former palaces, now being used as a hotel where visiting generals or colonels stayed. The grounds were lush and cool. Nearby was a river. Inside, the beds were comfortable and the food tasty and rich. I flew back to Al Asad, and a few weeks later Specialist Elizabeth Tice and I flew back to Baghdad for a conference. They wanted to put me in the same hotel, but Specialist Tice wasn't allowed because of her lower rank. I sweet-talked the guy on duty, and Specialist Tice was able to stay in the hotel with me. The conference went well and we even got out to do a little shopping. For a short time, things almost felt normal again. I wondered how I could translate this feeling back to Al Asad. I bought a big stuffed camel with a military hat and a huge gaudy neon picture of a deserted island surrounded by a tropical ocean. It had some kind of electronic deal where you could turn it on and see the waves moving. I brought the picture back to Al Asad, packed carefully in a huge duffel bag, and hung it on the wall in my CHU. The first night back, I turned off all the other lights, turned on the neon picture, and stared at the scene.

It reminded me of Tahiti, Bora Bora—George and I had traveled to both on vacation in happier times. All around my CHU, I glanced at my personal possessions—pictures of home, various other decorations, and stuffed animals, including Shaggy, whom I still took everywhere. The more I stared, the more homesick I felt. If I felt this way, I was sure others did, too. This would never do.

The next afternoon, the thermometer outside my CHU read 123 degrees. A real Daytona beach. I had a few off hours and took a walk around the base. Merav Brooks from HBO knew George from his interactions with the *Band of Brothers* miniseries, and she had sent me a whole container full of DVDs. I wasn't quite sure what to do with them, but my mind was working, trying to splice together all I was feeling with what needed to be done. I was still wrestling through things when I walked past the back of the dining facilities (DFAC). Two burly Alabama National Guardsmen were hanging out on a coffee break. The Guardsmen were charged with running the DFAC. I must have glanced in their direction and held my gaze just a little too long.

"Hey, buzz off," said one, a sergeant. He pointed to a sign beside the outside door that read, "Go away." He had a huge walrus mustache and thick hairy arms.

I stopped and stared at him coolly. "Buzz off yourself," I said back.

Slowly "Sergeant Walrus" grinned in my direction. I could tell his bark was worse than his bite. "Hey, you're all right, you know that," he said. "We don't get too many colonels behind the mess tent. Whaddya want anyway?"

"I don't know. Whaddya got?"

"Whadda we got?" He turned to the other sergeant and laughed. "She wants to know what we got." They both snorted. He turned to me. "Whadda *you* got—that's the real question."

"How's about a box full of HBO videos?" I said. "I got the *Sopranos, HBO World Championship Boxing, Deadwood, Sex and the City,* and about five copies of *Band of Brothers.* Interested?"

"Interested?" He glanced either way, then added under his breath, "Meet us back here in half an hour with a Humvee."

My mind was really rolling now. I headed over to the PX and bought a grill, the biggest one I could find, then lugged it back to my CHU.

Captain Diamond was just heading over for her shift and saw my load. She always worked second shift. I worked first. "What's going on, Sue?" she asked.

"What time's your dinner break tonight?"

"The usual. How come?"

"Never mind. Just meet me back here during dinner break. Bring anybody you can find. Come hungry."

I rounded up a Humvee and headed back over to the sergeants at the DFAC.

"You got the stuff?" said Sergeant Walrus.

"Yeah," I said. "You got the goods?"

"Out of the way," he said. "We'll load 'em up for you."

That night I assembled the grill in front of my CHU and fired it up. The warm, smoky smell of a backyard cookout filled the nighttime air. Anytime anyone got off shift, he or she had to pass by the grill on the way back to the CHUs. It didn't take long for word to spread. Soon, all around me were smiles and laughter. From the stash provided by the sergeants, I piled the grill with fresh hot dogs and flaming cheeseburgers—as many as anyone could eat. The sergeants had provided it all for us—meat, cheese, buns, ketchup, relish, fresh lettuce, tomatoes, and onions. If it was going to be as hot as Daytona Beach in Al Asad, then we were going to have a barbecue! Things almost felt normal again, if only for a little while. After grilling up about 20 burgers, I turned the grill over to Lieutenant Colonel Gary Grossi, a good friend. He was the psych nurse on base, and we worked together a lot. Captain Diamond settled back on the chair next to me and bit into her burger.

"You know, Sue," she said, "this is really living. We should do this every night except tomorrow night."

"That's a peach of an idea," I said. "But why not tomorrow night?"

"Because tomorrow I'm flying to Disney World."

"Michelle! I completely forgot. It's the big one, too, isn't it?"

"Yep, the big 5-0. Or 49, I guess—that's what I'll be telling everybody."

She was just kidding about going to Disney World. We both laughed. The next day, I drove the Humvee to the DFAC and knocked on the back door.

"You again?" said Sergeant Walrus. "Didn't I tell you to buzz off?"

"It's Dorothy and her little dog, Toto, from Kansas. We're here to see the Great Voice behind the screen."

"So it's classic movie references today, is it?" he said. "You got *Gone with the Wind?*"

"Nah, but I got three signed copies of Bill Guarnere and Babe Heffron's new book and three hats signed by Buck Compton."

He nodded. "More burgers?"

"Yeah. As many as you can give me. And I need a cake."

"A cake?"

"Yeah. A birthday cake. A big fancy one with lots of frosting."

"This is Iraq, Colonel. We ain't got no birthday cakes in Iraq."

"What about beer. You got any beer?"

"It's Iraq, I tell ya! You think I'd be standing here talking to you if we had any beer?"

"Well, do what you can do. I'll be back in a couple hours."

I don't know how they did it, and I never asked any specifics, but the sergeants of Oz were masters at their craft. That night to celebrate Captain Diamond's 50th birthday, we set up the grill, barbecued hamburgers, and feasted on the biggest birthday cake I had ever seen. Each person who passed us joined in the party. It was still 100 degrees even after the sun set, and into each person's hand, whoever wanted one, we placed a frosty amber O'Doul's, the perfect addition to a backyard cookout. It might have been Iraq, but we even had beer—even if it was the nonalcoholic kind.

From then on, Dorothy and Toto became regulars at the DFAC. The trades became wilder—did the sergeants need a couch? A Persian rug? Some expedited medical exams maybe? Dorothy was a woman who could get things. Nobody asked where all the extra food came from, and I didn't tell. I should point out that this trading was legit in the sense that we didn't actually steal anything from the DFAC. I had to sign for whatever I took. Yet the bartering became a standing practice anytime I went there. Sometimes there were extras that would have gone to waste if I hadn't taken them. That's how we viewed it, anyway. We set up the grill as often as we could. Each weekend we held a big barbecue. It became a big block party. We strung up lights and decorations. The menu often varied. First Sergeant Shirley Martino became the main grillmaster. She had a loud voice and could really round up a group of people in no time. "Hey! Listen to your First Sergeant! Come on over for food!" she yelled. Lieutenant Colonel Vignone got Italian cheese and pepperoni sent to her from home in Federal Hill. Outback Steakhouse came to the base for a special occasion and provided dinner. We feasted on grilled marinated steaks with baked potatoes, butter, and sour cream, with chocolate tower cake for dessert. Afterward, there were still 160 steaks left over, and they all came to me. We cooked them up on the grill and took them to the hospital for any of the wounded soldiers who wanted one.

The parties, the little touch of normalcy, seemed to break down barriers. Then the people who needed some kind of song started coming to me. I sang for anybody who was having a bad day at work, anybody who didn't hear from home, anybody who needed some cheering up. And they started coming to my fellow nurses who also sang. We might have been seeing the most gruesome things imaginable during the day, but after shift we became nightingales, the songbirds of Iraq. In the midst of this chaos came friendship and togetherness. When life handed us sandstorms and heat, we threw a barbecue. We would sing and sing until our voices grew hoarse, until the darkness would leave, and until we could just see the hopeful rays of morning light.

CHAPTER 13

Shot, Wounded, Killed

THE AIR FELT LIKE a stifling blanket. I yawned, trying to force my eyes open. It hurt to move. I'm a light sleeper on the best of days. In Mosul, traffic blended together to form a steady background din, but in Al Asad, I heard every helicopter as it flew overhead in the night. That, and I missed George. How many months had it been? Three in Fort McCoy. Another five in Mosul. Three months here in Al Asad. We still had another four months to go before we headed home. We were beginning to feel that we were close to the end. The challenge was to remain vigilant and diligent and not get sloppy now. The stakes were too high.

By afternoon the thermometer beside my CHU read 149.5 degrees Fahrenheit. People fried eggs on the sidewalks as a joke. The blazing weather went on for days, then an avian flu was tracked to our egg supplier, and real eggs were banned. That put an end to the egg-frying experiments. The post imposed strict water conservation measures and prioritized water use. People sweated more and stank more. We had intermittent power outages throughout the base, and nobody could seem to pinpoint why. Fortunately, the hospital had its own generators and was largely unaffected.

Whenever possible, at two in the afternoon, I went to Lieutenant Colonel Gloria Vignone's office and phoned George. Her phone worked better than mine, and she didn't mind. Unfortunately, all too often, we were on "Code Rivercity," the code for a communications blackout that was imposed whenever a service member died. Under Rivercity, all the phone banks and Internet connections were shut down. It made sense. Say someone like Chris Manion died; as soon as I heard the news, I'd want to run and phone Donna. The army, however, wanted to make sure that such news was relayed through official channels because there's always the potential that someone could get sensitive information wrong. Sometimes there were many dead, and we were put on Rivercity for up to four days at a time.

The best temperatures came around sunrise when the air was almost cool. The light played with the sky and sand of the Syrian Desert of western Iraq. It made for some breathtaking panoramas. Our medical incinerator (where we burned everything from Band-Aids to bones) spewed out flame and smoke and added a surreal touch to the scene. Colonel Blansfield and I met before breakfast one day. He was happy about the barbecues and the positive effect they were having throughout the unit. We went through our regular agenda, then he gave a little grin. "I heard a sort of funny joke today from one of our nurse-anesthetists," he said.

"Sort of funny?" I asked.

"Well, there's too much truth to it to be really funny."

"Okay, I'm all ears."

"Combat trauma is like bananas," he said. "Do you know why?"

"Why."

"Because it comes in bunches."

I smiled bleakly. The colonel was right. It was too true to be funny.

That week the colonel's "joke" was especially too true to be funny. On Monday, a suicide bomber in Ramadi, just east of us, killed 27 people and wounded double that number. They were all area residents, so we got the civilian hospitals to take as many as they could. Tuesday, another bunch of wounded came to us, victims of IEDs. Wednesday, several people were wounded by sniper fire. Thursday, Iraqi police opened fire on a ten-year-old boy who failed to stop when ordered. He came in with a gunshot wound to his leg and a fracture. His uncle carried him to the hospital. The irony? His uncle was the police chief.

"I gotta get my guys to stop shooting everyone," the police chief said. "They're pretty loose with the rules of engagement."

Friday, a young marine sergeant was brought to us. He had been sweating in the field heat, so he had opened up his vest to cool off. The little opening was all it took, and a sniper shot him between his armor plates. The average human body has about 5.6 liters of blood in it, or about 12 units. Normally, you can lose about 2 liters of blood and still live, though you're in deep trouble. This marine had lost 3 liters, maybe more. It was hard to tell exactly. We gave him tons of blood—Lieutenant Colonel Vignone said 60 units. Nobody thought he was going to make it. We ran out of blood and put out a call for more volunteers. His buddies from his unit came in and rolled up their sleeves. About a hundred donated blood. I ran trips to the dining hall to grab soda and cookies for the soldiers. Our ICU and OR staff worked on him for about 72 hours straight before he stabilized enough to be evacuated to Germany. His buddies stood at attention as we carried him out through their ranks. They insisted on helping load him on the ambulance to the airfield. The soldier lived and was soon back at Bethesda Naval Hospital, functioning normally, playing checkers and chess with the other wounded patients.

The next week, a marine was rushed to us with 50 percent of his body covered with third-degree burns. One arm was gone. We got him stabilized enough to allow him to be transported to Germany, where he met up with a burn team from Brooke Army Medical Center who took him to San Antonio, Texas. Last we heard, he also lived.

That same week, there was a mortar strike in Ramadi on a soccer field, and four young children were flown to us at once. They couldn't have been more than five or six years old. The mothering instincts of female nursing staff took over, and these kids got pretty spoiled in a hurry. They soon all got transferred to local facilities, each piled high with bags of goodies.

A short time later, we received an eight-year-old boy and his uncle who came in after an IED blast. The boy's hands were badly mangled, but our ortho-surgeon, who has hand experience, was able to save the thumb and a finger on one hand.

The next day, we had a MASCAL with 11 patients from an Iraqi police checkpoint—9 Iraqis and 2 Americans. Three died, including one soldier. We ran four OR tables simultaneously with a two-hour backlog for surgery. Again we ran out of blood. We put out another call for whole blood on the base and had to stop the line at 40 donors. As the fallen soldier was carried out of the hospital, a spontaneous Angel Ceremony was held for him. People formed two columns facing inward, came to attention, and remained silent until the body was loaded out. We were put on Rivercity until the immediate family was notified.

Then came one of our strangest patients of all.

The call came over the loudspeakers. A chopper came in and landed. I was coming back from visiting another unit and saw the patient when they wheeled him in. He had a long nose and a furry body. He was all bandaged up and had the saddest eyes I'd ever seen.

"Surgery on a dog?" I wondered out loud. It was a German shepherd, one of the canine troops used to sweep vehicles and inspect cargo for explosives.

"That dog is an American soldier," said one of the handlers who had just gotten off the chopper. "He's got a Social Security number and a rank. His name is Sergeant Lex, and he's one of the best. Unfortunately, he's the lucky one. . ." His voice trailed off. "His handler didn't make it."

So that's why the dog was so sad. As well as being hurt, he had lost his master. The dog must have sensed it. Poor thing—he was in critical condition. When the bomb exploded, a piece of shrapnel went through his hindquarters. His mucus membranes were pale and he showed little saliva. As well as being dehydrated, he was in shock, probably bleeding internally. We put the dog in the CAT scanner—which caused a few suppressed smiles as people hoped out loud the dog wouldn't mind suffering such a humiliation—and called in a vet on base. The dog's spleen was in two pieces, so the vet, who was actually a horse doctor and admitted he wasn't fully familiar with dogs, operated together with one of our trauma surgeons to take the spleen out. Sergeant Lex lived and was evacuated shortly after. I thought about my husband's brother, Steve Luz, who had been a dog handler in Vietnam. Steve had always talked about his dog with such affection. The dog was his partner, a soldier who went through thick and thin with him. Now I understood what Steve meant.

ON MAY 16, I CELEBRATED my 57th birthday with a barbecue outside my CHU. We ate a beautiful cake crafted at the DFAC and drank cranberry juice in wineglasses. That night I was standing in the shower wondering where the years had gone when I felt a nickel-sized lump in my breast. Like women everywhere who go through this, I felt the initial stab of fear. I had undergone two breast biopsies earlier and knew there's always the risk of cancer, but for some reason I quickly seemed to float above the worry this time. Still, whenever you find a lump, you're supposed to tell your doctor and have a mammogram, and when I met with Major Deniece Barnet-Scott the next day, she examined me and told me to have it checked out quickly. The only problem was that none of the military hospitals in Iraq were equipped to do mammograms. The only place was in Germany.

The thought of flying to Germany made me more nervous than the lump in my breast. Flying in Iraq had proved to be spotty at the best of times. What with the crazy weather and constantly changing conditions of the insurgency, flying any-where of distance held huge uncertainties. I knew it was easier to fly out of Iraq than to fly back in. Plus, I didn't want to leave Al Asad. We had work to do. My right-hand assistant, Special-ist Tice, had gone home on R&R in early May and broken her ankle while back in the States. She was hobbling around on crutches at home, and we weren't sure if we'd ever get her back. I didn't want to leave the base without any representatives from public health.

Strangely, there was another reason I hesitated about going to Germany. George was going to be there. I wanted to see him, of course, but I didn't want anyone to think I was shirking my duty to go see my husband. Truly, that wasn't in my heart. Neither he nor I knew the exact dates we'd be there. He was helping on a *Band of Brothers* tour and would be somewhere in the area when I got there. World War II veterans Buck Compton, Don Malarkey, Frank Perconte, Rod Bain, Bill Guarnere, and Babe Heffron were all in Europe touring various military bases and hospitals to encourage the soldiers. The veterans were all in their mid-80s, so George and Rod Bain's daughter, Donna, were along to help the men navigate the tour.

Right about then, Lieutenant Colonel Vignone also found a lump in her breast, so now there were two of us who needed mammograms. She worked as head nurse in the intermediate care ward and was adamant about leaving.

"Look, you can't fool around with this stuff," she said.

Major General Silverman's directive was the clincher. He pulled me aside and said, "Look—you're going." He wasn't smiling. "So what if you meet up with your husband over there? You're going, even if I have to fly you there myself."

So Lieutenant Colonel Vignone and I flew out of Al Asad to the city of Balad, Iraq, where sandstorms delayed all connecting flights. We overnighted there, then the next morning found a medical flight on a big C-130 that was heading to Landstuhl, Germany, to the U.S. Army's medical installation. Balad could be a rough place. As our plane taxied down the runway, we saw tracer bullets heading in our direction from nearby snipers. "Go! Go! Go!" I yelled—as if the pilots could hear me. I'm sure they were more worried than I was. I scrunched my eyes tight as the plane roared into the sky. Getting shot at in a medical plane—now, that takes the cake.

It takes several hours to fly from Balad to Landstuhl. Lieutenant Colonel Vignone and I sat watching the patients for a while, just looking at these kids. We were sobered. Some sat on regular seats and were considered noncritical care. Others were in much worse shape, strapped to stretchers hooked to the floor. Nurses assigned to the wounded changed dressings and monitored IVs, same as in a ward. Some of the soldiers were badly burned. Others had lost legs. Some were unconscious. Once the plane was at cruising altitude, we walked around, meeting as many patients as we could, just trying to say small words of encouragement: "Hey, how you doing?" "Can we get you anything?" "Thanks for your service." In my nursing career I've spoken to a lot of patients over the years. Time and time again, the thing that impressed me about the soldiers we met was how polite they were. Guys would say, "I'm okay, but could you make sure you talk to my friend over there? He's having trouble." Or, "If it's not too much of a problem, would you be able to get me a drink of water?" They seemed so grateful for the smallest things we could do. The U.S. Army consists entirely of volunteers, and I was struck again with what a privilege it is to care for America's men and women in uniform.

We arrived in Landstuhl and were bused to the base. They put me in a fancy hotel, but Lieutenant Colonel Vignone was assigned to the barracks. I pulled some strings and got her a room in the hotel. On the first night, we went to a small German restaurant nearby. Feelings of guilt and pleasure swirled within me. The rest of our unit was taking care of wounded, responding to MASCALs, and fighting off mortar attacks, and we were feasting in leisure on *Cremeschnitte* and Heinekens. George and I tried to connect by phone, but all I learned was that he and the tour were about five hours away. Landstuhl was a scheduled stop on the tour, but only for a few hours, and no one knew exactly when. I wanted to see him so badly, but I dared not hope too hard. Inside, I felt confused and muddled.

Landstuhl is a huge medical facility, and Lieutenant Colonel Vignone and I had mammograms scheduled on different days. I had some time before my appointment, so I was able to meet the man who had been Chris Manion's command sergeant major back in Mosul and with whom I had talked several times there. The command sergeant major had been shot in the legs and was getting stabilized in Germany before being sent home to the States.

Our conversation allowed me to catch up on all the news from the other base. Chris was doing fine. The command sergeant major didn't much like the new medical unit that had replaced us. Previously, whenever one of his soldiers was wounded, he was able to come right into the ER to see how the man was doing, but the new unit wouldn't let him do that. He thanked us again for our flexibility.

I had my mammogram; something didn't look right on it, which triggered a biopsy, which meant another couple of days in Germany. Again, I didn't worry about the procedure. I knew in my heart I was going to be okay. I also knew now that there was a very good chance I'd be able to meet George. Sure enough, a day later, it happened.

"George!"

"Susan!"

There he was in the hospital. I couldn't believe it! As we ran to each other, I was caught by a wave of emotion. His hug and kiss told me he was real. What were the chances of this? How could this be—that I was in Germany during a war with my husband next to me?

I caught my breath and introduced Lieutenant Colonel Vignone to all the veterans, unable to take my eyes off George. All too soon, the men began their hospital tour. The members of the Band of Brothers are celebrities in military circles. They toured all over the hospital, meeting patients, encouraging the wounded, passing out gifts, signing autographs. The patients were so excited to see them. Someone saw my name tag and asked me if George Luz Sr. was my father. "No, but George Luz Jr. is my husband," I said, and beamed.

It was a short visit. George and I quickly kissed good-bye, and the tour continued to another base. As soon as they left, the uneasy feeling returned and now, more than ever, I wanted to get the heck out of Germany and back to Iraq and finish my job.

Both tests came back negative, meaning the lump I had felt was benign. We were relieved. We caught a flight on a regular transport to Ramstein, Germany, where we had a layover. The wait lasted for hours. Kuwait was having sandstorms, so we chose another route and caught a plane as far as Qatar, an Arab emirate on the northern coast of Saudi Arabia. The humidity and heat were terrible in Qatar, where we were stuck for three days waiting for a final flight back to Al Asad. Finally, we got onboard and made it back. It was a strange irony to be so happy to be back in a war zone. We had been away from Al Asad for two full weeks. The first night back, Toby Keith, the country-and-western star, held a USO concert in the old decrepit soccer stadium on base and was a big hit. His patriotic-near-redneck-all-American music must have been just what everyone needed, because there were huge smiles all around. It was also a moment to mark time. We had mobilized a year ago and now had 100 days to the finish line of our time in this country.

After the concert, it was business as usual. The UH-60 Army Blackhawk medevac birds and Marine CH-46 Sea Knight twin rotor helicopters landed the next morning, bringing more wounded. We were hit with a nine-patient detainee MASCAL—all bad guys. None were hurt seriously, so they were cleared quickly and taken to a detainee facility.

I CALLED THE PERKY, attractive sergeant Marilyn Monroe, but her actual name was Marilyn Mauro. One afternoon we were out in one of the intensive care canisters, the place where stuff is stored before it's taken into the hospital. We worked to unload equipment from the roof of a medical supply van into the canister.

Sergeant Mauro was standing on one box, stretching for another large box she couldn't quite reach. I was down below, set to take the box from her when she brought it down.

"Hey, Marilyn," I said. "You got your lipstick and high heels on? Maybe that would help you reach it."

"Yeah, yeah," she said. "Hang on a sec. I'll get it."

"Let me give you a hand."

"Nah, it's light as a feather." There was a grating sound. A small rivulet of sawdust trickled from the box. It gave a little jerk, then slipped. "Watch out!" she yelled. It was too late. The box came crashing down on my arm and I crumpled to the floor.

"Auuuuugh!" I hollered. It felt as if my arm was clamped in a vise. "It's my wrist. I think it's broken." The pain was so intense that I was crying.

Sergeant Mauro jumped to my side instantly. We could see now that the box was full of sawdust—the kind used to absorb spills on floors. "Oh, I'm so sorry! I'm so sorry! I'm so sorry," she repeated. She was crying, too.

I looked at her and grimaced. "What the heck are you crying for?" I said. "It's my arm that's broken."

That made her choke a little and grin at herself. I started chuckling and she started chuckling back. We would have been laughing out loud except that my arm hurt so much. It was another crazy mixture of feelings.

Sergeant Mauro helped me over to the hospital. As we approached, people saw I had been crying and ran to me. "Colonel Luz? What's wrong? Are you okay?" I felt like a big baby.

They gave me a shot of morphine right away, then took X-rays. Sure enough, it was a broken wrist. They wanted to keep me overnight in the hospital for observation, but I wanted to be back in my own bed and insisted on leaving. They put a cast on my arm that reached all the way to my collarbone and sent me back to my CHU with a morphine drip. The drip leaked all over, so the next morning I went back to the hospital and had them take it out. That was the last morphine I took. Colonel Paul Astphan met me in the hospital. He was our executive officer, the number two of the unit, and a great guy. His face looked grave.

"You know, you really need to go recuperate in Qatar," he said. "Although it's really Colonel Kelly's decision."

"I don't want to go," I said. "I was just gone to Germany. If I leave now, I'll never return."

"Well, you need to go see Colonel Kelly. I wish I could do more."

So I went to see Colonel Kelly. "Sue, you're out of here," he said, quietly but firmly. "You need to go heal." He was looking out for my welfare, but I didn't see it that way.

"No way," I said. "I'm staying."

"Take it up with higher headquarters, then," Colonel Kelly said, and I agreed. Later on that day, Colonel Kelly placed the call to the general for me.

"General Silverman," I pleaded over the phone. "I can't leave. My specialist is out with a broken ankle. We're in the middle of an anthrax immunization drive. We're just getting ready to start the postdeployment health assessments. No one can get out of the country without those. We've got work to do. I've got to finish what I started."

He hemmed and hawed. "I don't know, Colonel," he said.

I pleaded my case again. I simply couldn't leave.

For me, it was the same feeling I had back in the Peace Corps. I knew that if I left before the job was finished, the challenge would have beaten me. That's why I went back to Quixadá after being assaulted. That's why I wanted to stay in Iraq. I didn't tell

General Silverman all that history, but I kept pleading and he finally agreed. I will be forever grateful to those two men.

I went right back to work with my arm in a sling. Master Sergeant Kim Luce and Captain Barbara Webster helped me get ready in the morning. Others helped me type reports. My friends knew how badly I wanted to stay. They knew if I couldn't do my job I'd be shipped out. I continued my work with the expectants and the immunizations. I upped my teaching schedule and taught health classes on weight control, sexually transmitted diseases, smoking cessation, and hygiene. I continued going out each day and visiting the various units. I talked to the soldiers. I brought them DVDs and books from home. I took them pizzas and soda pop. We kept up with our barbecues back at my CHU. My schedule grew busier, not lighter, even with the broken wrist.

And I dreamed up a new way for boosting morale on base. In some ways, the marine base at Al Asad could be tougher than others. Marines tend to foster the reputation for toughness. For instance, you needed to be in full uniform in Al Asad at all times. But I figured that anything to help the soldiers' morale was necessary—particularly the female soldiers. As time went on, I developed a more urgent burden to help out my sisters in arms. There's something incredibly poignant about seeing a wounded male soldier, a young American man cut down in the prime of his life, but to see a wounded female soldier—one of our country's daughters lying hurt—that nearly took my heart away.

So it might not sound like much, but I started a beauty salon on base. I first needed to convince the marine general that it was worthwhile. I explained the plan, and he looked at me like I was a nut job. There are a lot of women on base, I noted—whatever helps them get through each day was worth it. He shrugged and granted permission. I got permits and secured Turkish contractors to run it. When the inspections were over, the salon opened and did a steady business from that moment onward. I got my nails done and my gray hair dyed blond again. The general came by to see how the salon was doing. The military has a tradition of giving out honor coins, small tokens that commemorate worthwhile acts. The general inspected the salon, talked with a few of the patrons, then presented me an honor coin. That came as a real shock.

"This is for opening up a beauty salon?" I asked, surprised.

"No," he said. "It's because you truly care for my troops."

RIGHT AFTER I BROKE my arm, I got a nighttime knock on the door of my CHU. I glanced at my clock—3:15 A.M. The knocking grew louder.

"Colonel Luz!"

I opened the door. It was Captain Michelle Diamond. Still working second shift, she often came to my room about midnight. We'd laugh together, tell stories, and debrief each other on events of the day. But something was wrong. She was standing by the door, crying uncontrollably. "It's my sister," said Captain Diamond. "I just got word from home. She could go at any time."

"Don't worry," I said. "I can get you there."

The immediate concern was getting a flight back to the States as quickly as possible. I pulled some strings, and Captain Diamond flew out the next morning. Her sister was battling leukemia and lymphoma. She lingered for a short time after Captain Diamond flew home, then died. She was only in her early 50s. Captain Diamond came back to Iraq, obviously grieving, but happy she had gotten to see her sister one last time.

The little things about my job always seemed to do the most good, like helping Captain Diamond secure the flight home.

I was proud that I had made the decision to stay. I got my cast off after eight weeks and then wore a brace on my arm.

Soon after the salon opened, Colonel Blansfield received a very sad phone call about a female soldier, a call that helped fuel my fire to finish strong. Army Captain Maria Ines Ortiz, 40, had been killed in Baghdad by indirect fire. She was the first nurse to die from combat injuries in the Iraq War, and the first army nurse to die in combat since Vietnam. Ortiz was caring for wounded Iraqis at a hospital inside the fortified district known as the Green Zone, supposedly a safe place, when the hits came from a complex attack of mortars and rockets.

I had met Captain Ortiz a month earlier. She was fluent in both English and Spanish, same as me, and we joked around in Spanish together. She was also a twin, I remembered, as I have some sets of twins in my extended family. She smiled a lot, and I liked that. She seemed so genuinely passionate about her work caring for others.

Colonel Blansfield flew to the memorial service to represent the 399th. He described the service as somber and moving. People told how Captain Ortiz was a person of conviction, how she went to Iraq not because of the war, but because of a sense of mission. She volunteered because she wanted to make a difference. Just as the service broke up, another attack occurred on the Baghdad base, and attendees at the funeral were in lockdown under cover for more than an hour until the all-clear signal. Mortars hit the helicopter landing zone, the motor pool, generators, and the housing area, but thankfully there were no additional injuries.

"I had memories of being in Mosul again," Colonel Blansfield told me when he returned. He gave a little nod and shuffled some papers on his desk. All the color was drained from his face as if he had been on a long trip that wasn't quite over yet. "It could have been any of us, shot, wounded, or killed. That's for sure. Any of us."

CHAPTER 14

My Own Star

SEPTEMBER 2007: WE HAD three weeks left in Iraq. A new unit came to replace us, and we trained them for two weeks, then turned over our hospital to them. We packed up our belongings and moved into tents so that the new unit could move into our CHUs. People began to mail items home, as we were authorized only two duffels each to take with us. We held one last big blowout, a big cookout with a Hawaiian theme. Right in the middle of barbecued hamburgers, the helicopters arrived with incoming wounded. The war didn't take a break for anything.

With the new unit trained, it meant one week to go with time on our hands. For the first time in 16 months, there was almost nothing for our unit to do. Most people worked out or read. It was a little cooler in the season now, and though tanning was against regulations, I decided I wanted to look a little better before I went home to my husband, so I sat out in the sun. While I was outside my tent, some loudmouth came by and told me off: "Hey—that's punishable with an article 15."

"What are they going to do about it?" I quipped. "Send me to Iraq?" I kept tanning.

Then it was time to go home.

Exact dates or times for flying anywhere are seldom issued

with much advance notice in the army. When our last day came, we waited near the airport for a window to leave. One came, we headed for the tarmac, loaded the planes, and left. It was as simple as that.

I volunteered to leave on the last plane out. I'm not exactly sure why. Maybe I wanted to do as thorough a job as possible, to be the last one out the door—that sort of feeling. We flew to Kuwait for one night, then on to Shannon, Ireland, then back to the United States. Captain Diamond was with me on this flight, and as I'd done on the way over, I gave up my first-class seat so I could go back and sit with her. We talked nonstop about what we had just been through. As we descended for a stopover in Maine, we fell silent and looked out. That piece of home turf looked so good. On the ground, Captain Diamond and I ate lobster salad, our first taste of East Coast cuisine in more than a year. We continued the flight on to Wisconsin and Fort McCoy. I couldn't believe the cool temperatures, the clean, fresh fall air. A warm, gentle rain was falling when we landed in Wisconsin, and I stood still and let it fall on my face. I closed my eyes in something close to a prayer. It was a pleasure even to breathe in this country.

The first thing we did at McCoy was turn in our weapons. My revolver had been by my side constantly for the past 16 months. Without it, I almost panicked at first. Something vital felt missing from my person. For so long, we had not been able, ever, to walk around without our body armor and helmets. Now it almost felt like I didn't have any clothes on, yet there was also a wash of relief at shedding the extra weight and knowing I didn't need weapons or protective gear here.

With so many units coming and going, it took a week for us to debrief at McCoy. The days were busy with a drone of activity that felt almost anticlimactic. We each took a physical and a hearing test. Doctors said I had lost part of my hearing from all the mortars in Mosul. I hadn't counted on that. I knew my broken wrist would heal, but it was surprising to learn there would be permanent physical repercussions from my time in Iraq. I would process the feelings gradually in the months to come.

An awards ceremony was held on our last night at McCoy. It felt a bit like graduation. It was a pretty quick thing, considering that there were nearly 450 people going through it. Names were called alphabetically, and awards were announced individually. Both the command sergeant major and commander shook hands with each person whose name was called. The recipients said thank you, walked across the stage, and were done.

As the announcer called out those whose last names began with L, I heard the words "Colonel Luz, Bronze Star." My mouth fell open. I felt myself walking across the stage and reaching out my hand to receive my award. My feelings went into a tailspin of numbness. I knew that a Bronze Star is awarded for bravery, acts of merit, or heroic service. It's the fourth-highest combat award of the U.S. Armed Forces and the ninth-highest military award (including both combat and noncombat awards) in the order of precedence of U.S. military decorations. It's not given out lightly. All this went through my mind as I took the few steps down from the platform.

In a conversation later with General Silverman, I asked him why a public health nurse would ever get such an award. "I really don't understand. You get the Bronze Star for jumping out of airplanes and saving people," I said.

"No," said the general. "You get it for outstanding work. That's why you got it, Colonel Luz."

The awards ceremony took place on a Sunday night. It began raining toward the end—hard rain this time—and I ran back to my barracks to stow my gear in preparation for heading out the next morning for Hanscom Air Force Base. It was a strange sort of triumph. I was happy, yes, but all I could think of was that nurse who got killed in Iraq—Captain Maria Ines Ortiz. Now she was buried in Arlington. I was thankful for the award I received, I truly was, but my thought was that people like Captain Ortiz did the real heavy lifting in Iraq, and she, not I, deserved the Bronze Star.

We flew back to Hanscom on October 2, 2007, and marched into a hangar where relatives and friends waited with balloons, yellow roses, homemade signs, and American flags. A thunderous applause greeted us. I looked around, not quite knowing what to do. Some soldiers fought back tears. Some beamed with excitement. Many people in the crowd wept openly. We weren't allowed to greet our family members just yet. Another big ceremony came first. I scanned the crowd. I could just make out George near the back of the room. I bit my lip. He was looking somewhere else, probably trying to find me.

The ceremony started. One by one, dignitaries welcomed us home. We fidgeted in our chairs. I had trouble concentrating on what was being said. I kept seeing a succession of faces in my mind as if they were part of an honor review—an angry Iraqi police chief carrying his wounded son into the hospital; my nephew, Geoffrey, who was still fighting his own war at home; a corporal whose name I can't recall winning the battle for morale by frying eggs on the Iraqi tarmac; a bandaged child clutching a goody bag heading out on a helicopter.

About 50 minutes into the ceremony, First Sergeant Shirley Martino, my good buddy and grillmaster back at Al Asad, could wait no longer. As a band played, she jumped up from the front row and ran to the back of the hangar, yelling, "Come here,

I'll hug you! Sixteen months! Come on." She wrapped herself around her two daughters and lifted her little grandson off the ground. Finally, Colonel Kelly said the words we were all waiting to hear: "Task force dismissed." A roar filled the hangar as soldiers and families rushed toward one another. I embraced George, closed my eyes, and stood for several minutes in silence, running my hands across his back under his sport coat. Finally I opened my eyes.

"I'm home," I said.

MY SISTER THREW a big party with friends and family. On a bedsheet in the driveway hung a big sign that read, "Welcome home, Susie." When we got inside the house, there was a lot of hugging and laughter. In some ways it felt like I had never left. Later, when George and I drove home, my whole street was lined with American flags. Neighbors really went all out to welcome me home. I felt proud that I had done my duty and honored that so many people in my neighborhood felt that way, too. Back at our house, I found that George had renovated the whole master bedroom while I was gone. He had gutted the upstairs and everything new was installed. Local businesspeople had offered to help George when they learned of the project. Area contractors and a whole list of people pitched in. Really, it was a gift to me from the whole community. It was a wonderful way to come home.

Within just a few days, I went back to my job working with teenagers at Gateway Healthcare. It's an acute residential treatment center, a 24-hour lockdown facility, a step down from hospitalizations. We work with adolescents ages 12 to 18 with severe psychological problems. They're often suicidal, even homicidal. I'm the nurse case manager there. It's another stressful job—sometimes kids need to be in restraints, sometimes they smear feces all around, sometimes they spit at you and try to hit you. But I feel right at home there with Dr. Savitzky and the great team I work with. It's just part of what I do, part of who I am.

Our reserve unit met again in a month. Everyone caught up on all the news. Some people weren't adjusting to life at home very well. Some were in counseling. Some were simply not sleeping. There were a few divorces. Me—whenever I heard loud noises I got startled, but that was about it. I went and got it checked out at the Veterans Administration, and they said, "You're pretty normal."

"Yeah," I said. "I was nutty before I left."

Today, almost two years after returning from Iraq, not a day goes by that I don't think about my time in the war zone. I don't dwell on it, but I can't forget the injuries we saw. The faces. The lives. The people. In our year in the Mideast, our unit treated more than 30,000 wounded, endured 300 mortar attacks, and handled 14 MASCAL situations. We saw everything from soldiers missing limbs to civilians blown up at a car dealership. I will never shake those images.

But I can't forget the good parts as well: The adventure. The service. The cookouts in front of the CHU. My time in Germany with George that came as such a surprise. My friendship and camaraderie with so many in the unit. The real and purposeful work that was done.

As I write these last few pages, the war in Iraq is not over. I have no great predictions for how the conflict is going to end, but I hope and pray that lasting peace, stability, and liberty will be brought to that country. We continue to hear news reports of improvements in the region, and we continue to hope for the best.

As for my responsibilities with the Army Reserves, I have volunteered to go on a medical mission to Guatemala in a few months. The work continues.

Just after this book releases in 2010, I'll celebrate my 60th birthday and my 25th wedding anniversary. I'm eligible to stay in the reserves until I'm 62, but I don't know—I'm thinking of retiring soon. I want to do some more traveling, see more of the world: Australia, the Orient, maybe Bora Bora again. I want to travel with George and grow old with him. I want to enjoy more of life with my friends and family at home, to be a wife and auntie. I don't want to run off and go to another war. But if one were to break out, I would have no qualms about going. I wouldn't be first in line to volunteer, but I'd be proud to serve. I always have been, and I always will be.

I continue to hope for a cure for Cystic Fibrosis. I don't want to outlive my nephews. I pray for them every day. They're fighting a different kind of war. Some days they win some battles. Some days the battles are all uphill.

Young Chris Manion came home from Iraq safely and in one piece. He married his sweetheart, Jennifer, near Christmastime and is back in the States still on active duty. George and I went to the wedding, as proud as could be of the good decisions this young man continues to make.

Looking back, my life has been wonderful, really. It's had its ups and downs, but I keep in mind my mother's words: "There's always going to be someone worse off than you." That perspective has helped me through many situations. "If something hard happens, you pick yourself up and keep going," Mom said. I can't go back in time, so I strive to live each day the best it can be. My aim always is to give myself to the people I meet, to serve others in wholeheartedness. Serving others has been my life's priority, and the blessing has been mine. The more you give, the more you get. That's the purpose I've found in life. That's the nightingale's song I always want to sing.

On the first Veteran's Day after returning from Iraq, George and I went to visit my parents' graves, as my father was a veteran, then over to see the grave site of Brian St. Germain, George's cousin's son who was killed on his second tour in Iraq. George's dad, a veteran of World War II, is buried in the same cemetery. The sun was shining brightly although it was early November, and the leaves listed down with their reds, oranges, golds, and yellows. We placed flowers on Brian's grave and stood silently in tribute, then walked to George's dad's grave and did the same. Together, George and I offered up a prayer of thanksgiving for their service. The nurses and doctors in Iraq and our other wars took care of a lot of wounded and saved a lot of lives, but unfortunately not all were saved. This high price is what we can never forget. There at the grave sites, I heard a bird sing. Its voice was clear and brilliant, and I swear it sounded just like a nightingale.

❖

APPENDIX: OFFICER'S EVALUATION REPORT

EVALUATION REPORT FOR:
Luz, Susan P.
399th CSH w/duty in Iraq

EVALUATORS:
Kelly, Bryan R., TF 399th Commander
Silverman, Ronald D., Commanding General

SIGNIFICANT DUTIES AND RESPONSIBILITIES:
Responsible for promoting, protecting, optimizing, and preserving the health and abilities of approximately 17,000 U.S. and coalition service members as well as 10,000 civilians through the delivery of community health services. Duties include but are not limited to: immunizations, smoking cessation, PDHAs, R&R redeployment briefing, weight counseling, STD counseling and contract tracing, and health promotion classes as requested. Additional duties include mental health nursing in support of combat stress as required.

COMMENT ON SPECIFIC ASPECTS OF PERFORMANCE:
COL Susan Luz led from the front throughout the deployment demonstrating initiative and selfless service. She instituted community health programs, in conjunction with preventative medicine assets, at FOB Diamondback, MND-North, Mosul and Al Asad AFB, MNF-West, Iraq. COL Luz was the primary asset in

planning, coordinating, and participating in a community health fair for FOB Marez East and West in Mosul, Iraq, during November of 2006. She supervised an influenza immunization clinic for the soldiers on Marez with 100 percent compliance, as well as the anthrax immunization program for TF 399th CSH in Al Asad, again with 100 percent compliance. MNC-I Surgeon Cell solicited COL Luz as a trainer in the community health arena, presenting at the Baghdad Preventative Medicine Conference in January 2007 on the importance of community health nursing services in the deployed environment. She was a guest speaker representing TF 399th CSH at the Al Asad Women's History Month program presenting a well-received oration on Women in the Military. COL Luz was recognized by the Commander of the 1st Cavalry in Mosul with a Commander's Coin for her outstanding work in support of soldier combat stress management.

COMMENT ON PERFORMANCE/POTENTIAL:

COL Luz has done an outstanding job for TF 399th CSH and TF 3d MEDCOM, ensuring the preventive health care of all soldier and MND-N and MNF-W during OIF 06–08. Her skill sets in community health and mental health have been a force multiplier in theater and critical to the success of the command's mission. COL Luz's compassion and total dedication to soldier health is second to none. Her ability to network in a joint-multinational force environment fostered the integration of the first Level III Combat Support Hospital in MNF-W, Al Asad, Iraq. COL Luz is a well-respected veteran in the Army Nurse Corps, who has represented the United States Army Reserve with integrity, honor, and loyalty during her current mobilization in a combat environment.

ACKNOWLEDGMENTS

IN A LETTER TO Major Dick Winters, Sergeant Mike Ranney wrote that his grandson had asked, "Grandpa, were you a hero in the war?"

"No," Mike Ranney answered the boy, "but I was in a company of heroes."

He signed the letter to Major Winters, "Your Easy Company Comrade."

This is how this book started for me. My father-in-law, George Luz Sr., was portrayed in Stephen Ambrose's book *Band of Brothers*. Later, the story was turned into an HBO miniseries produced by Tom Hanks and Steven Spielberg. Greg Johnson from the WordServe Literary Group read a newspaper article about my time in Iraq and knew about my connections to the Band of Brothers. He approached my husband, George, and me about me writing about my experiences overseas.

Privately, I told myself no way, as I was sure that everyone in my unit would have better stories to tell than I did. Anyway, if I did write about my life, I wanted to make the story about more than my experiences in Iraq. My life is not just about my 26 years in the Army Reserve Nurse Corps (even though I think of every one of my soldiers as heroes); my life is about my family and friends, serving overseas with the Peace Corps and with Project HOPE, and my career as a nurse for more than 37 years. It is especially about my life as a wife and aunt who dedicates her time to her nieces and nephews. I was single when all three of my nephews were born with cystic fibrosis, and I determined I would always be there for them. They, like my sisters and brothers in war, are also my heroes.

In the end, I decided to write this book as a way to pay tribute to the heroes I've known throughout my life. Everyone I know has always said to me, "Oh, what a life you've had! You should write a book." So that's how this book started.

In the process of writing a book, there are so many people to thank. To begin, I want to thank my editor, Shannon Berning, and the team at Kaplan for championing this book from the start. Thanks to Greg, my agent, and my collaborative writer, Marcus Brotherton. I met Marcus at Lieutenant Buck Compton's first book signing in Seattle. Marcus had cowritten a book called *Call of Duty*, about one of my father-in-law's buddies, and I said to myself that Marcus was not only a great writer but also a great guy.

Over the last few months, Marcus drew me back in time to recall memories and stories along the way. I found the process more difficult than I first imagined. I have so many good memories, but some memories I've definitely tried to forget. So this is not a tell-all book by any means, but a slice of my life as it relates to the greater theme of service. For those who know me well, you know that there are some chapters of my long life journey that I've chosen to leave out. In the end, I feel comfortable with what I have shared. I love my life now more than ever.

I'd like to recognize some of the people who helped mold me and who I admire for making a difference in my life and accepting me for who I am. Let me start with some of my army buddies. Wild Bill Guarnere and Edward Babe Heffron are two of my oldest friends; they served with my husband's dad in the

101st Airborne, 506th, E Company. They call me "the broad," but I know it is a form of endearment.

Then there is my own "Band of Sisters": Lieutenant Colonel Elaine D'Antuono, Captain Michele Diamond, Colonel Deniece Barnett-Scott, Captain Bertha Maloof, First Sergeant Shirley Martino, Master Sergeant Kim Luce, Lieutenant Colonel Gloria Vignone, Lieutenant Colonel Debbie Barrette, Major Yvonne Ivanov, Lieutenant Colonel Colleen Kloehn, and Major Carliss Towne. Thanks for all the memories.

Colonel Paul "Paulie" Astphan, Colonel Joseph "Joey Boy" Blansfield, Colonel Joaquin "J. C." Cortiella, Colonel Marty Phillips, Colonel Greg "Quickie" Quick, and Colonel Bob "Tabby Cat" Tabaroni—I want to thank you for always letting me be part of your boys' club. Thanks as well to Colonel Mike "Kojak" Kolodziej and Major Rick Bailey, who even gave in at the end. I love you all! Also, a special recognition to Colonel Maureen Holland, Lieutenant Colonel Carolyn Bannon, Colonel Judy Haseltine, and Colonel Joyce Humphrey.

Thanks to Major General Ronald D. Silverman, my mentor in Iraq, for all you did for me and my troops, as well as the soon-to-be Brigadier General Bryan Kelly, my 399th Combat Support Hospital Commander, Brigadier General Oscar DePriest from the 804th Hospital Command, Major General Dean Sienko, my flying partner, Brigadier General Jonathan Woodson, Major General Michael Stone, Lieutenant Jack Stultz, and Lieutenant General Reggie Centracchio.

I have met some extraordinary commissioned and noncommissioned officers over the years, and here are only a few: Major Diane Adloff, Captain Carol Agostini, Sergeant First Class Ray Arbrige, Sergeant First Class Adolfo Becerril, Lieutenant Colonel Mary Bolk, the boys from the Alabama National Guard, Major Doug

Chung, Sergeant First Class David Cirella, Sergeant First Class Bruce Courage, Colonel Eddy Cyr, Lieutenant Colonel David Dehaas, Lieutenant Colonel Father John Doran, Lieutenant Mike Douglas, Specialist Tara Edminston, Lieutenant Colonel Mike Feldman, Captain Nick Fox, Captain Chris Gardiner, Command Sergeant Major Ray Gomez, Major Doral Gonzales, Lieutenant Colonel Gary Grossi, Colonel Judy Haseltine, Lieutenant Colonel Emily Heath, Colonel Maureen Holland, Colonel Joyce Humphrey, Major Kathy Kiesa, Major Heidi Kelly, Sergeant First Class Mike King, Major Joseph Kline, Sergeant First Class Rick Levesque, Captain Chris Manion, Sergeant First Class Marilyn Mauro, Major Casey Miner, Sergeant Chuck O'Donnell, Sergeant First Class Robert Rayne, Lieutenant Colonel Rene Remillard, Major Kristie Saunders, Sergeant First Class Robert Sliker, Command Sergeant Major David Smith, Major Paula Smith, Captain Tiffany Sockwell, Captain David Soderlund, Sergeant Domingo Soto-Santana, Specialist Elizabeth Tice, Colonel Stephen Twitty, Staff Sergeant Angel Vega, Lieutenant Colonel Eric Welch, Command Sergeant Major James Pippen and all the Cavalry at Fort Bliss, Lieutenant David Villarroel, Captain Barbara Webster, Master Sergeant Glen Weyland, Sergeant First Class Erich Zink, Sergeant Jonathan Alicea, Specialist Loralyn Bemis, Sergeant Carlos Bento, Sergeant Moshe Mayfield, Sergeant Russell McGillivray, First Sergeant Charlie Boisseau, Sergeant Matthew Caiazzo, Sergeant Nicole Chadbourne, Sergeant Rebekah Chiarini, Major Gail Christianson, Sergeant John Clinton, Sergeant Oleen Millette, Sergeant Scott Moreau, First Lieutenant Michelle Nesselroad, Lieutenant Colonel Michael Nott, Captain Edward Noyes, Major Terri Ohlinger, Sergeant Bryan O'Rourke, Lieutenant Colonel Jeffrey Pascale, Colonel Tony Pasqualone, Sergeant Karen Deraps, Captain Rita Ed, First

Lieutenant Ellen Elliott, Sergeant Susan Featherstone, Specialist John Flood, First Sergeant Bill Pierce, Sergeant Matthew Powell, Sergeant Michael Reed, Corporal Ian Rollins, Lieutenant Colonel Diana Hoek, Major Michael Grasso, Major Ken Grundy, Captain Michelle Jacobs, Sergeant Andy Jeanbaptiste, Staff Sergeant Paul Jodrey, Sergeant James Tilton, Specialist Ben Snowman, Major John Twomey, Lieutenant Colonel Geraldine Kass, Staff Sergeant Andrew Kyere, Master Sergeant Dale Lambert, Sergeant Andrew Lankford, Captain Robert Laskey, First Lieutenant Diana Libby, Lieutenant Colonel Joseph Luz, Captain Bruce Wheeler, Staff Sergeant Kirk Wolloff, Sergeant Brian Yeager, Specialist Allison Yeager, Major Paul Zaborski, Captain Stacey York, Specialist Jamie Zitterkopf, Captain Jamie Asaiante, Major Carol Voccio, Captain Gloria Bhoge, Major Arlene Mayotte, Captain Beverly Bourbonniere, Captain Macgregor Morgan, Major Michael Moulding, Colonel Beth Mazych, Major Leslie Carlson, Sergeant Amanda Cataldo, Lieutenant Colonel Robert Moore, Specialist Quyen Pham, Sergeant Judy Phothimath, Sergeant Jamie Hipp, Captain Richard Huff, Captain Rebecca Scheible, Specialist Patricia Thomas, Captain Maria Silva, Specialist Chris Harding, the late Sergeant Mike Skoczen, Major Valiant Lyte, Staff Sergeant Nathan McMannus, Lieutenant Colonel Marcia Aupperlee, Lieutenant Colonel Mike Alexander, Master Sergeant Charles Michaud, Sergeants Lisa and Steven McCullough, Master Sergeant Donna Cirella, the late Specialist Robert Motika, Captain Kevin Murphy, Sergeant Matt Bloom, Sergeant Mike Skocze, Lieutenant Colonel Mike Brown, Staff Sergeant Islande Cadichon, Major Dennis Callender, Lieutenant Colonel Jack Banford, Lieutenant Colonel Chiccarelli, Specialist Dan Palacios, Specialist Alicia Rosenbaum, Sergeant Vivianne Rico, Specialist Tim Rochefort, Captain Jeremy Brooks, Sergeant Ean

Pierre, First Lieutenant Jeff Asper, Sergeant Ashley Crawford, First Sergeant Bob Bennett, Sergeant Kelvin Foye, Captain Jen Callahan, Sergeant First Class Kaye Karlsen, Sergeant First Class Kevin Parrish, Sergeant Laura Kostura, Captain Deb Galewski, Lieutenant Colonel Joseph Osmanski, Lieutenant Colonel Lorie Cornell, Specialist Mike Hines, First Lieutenant Victoria Townsend, Specialist John Lebhertz, Captain Cathy Linowski, Master Sergeant Walter Diaz, Command Sergeant Major Marissa Lopes, Colonel Audrey Hines, Major Susan Kamataris, Sergeant Richard Burns, Lieutenant Colonel James Weeden, Sergeant Richard O'Shea, Sergeant Tony Morey, Captain Linda Pascale, Lieutenant Colonel Betty Lou Terry, Captain Karen Herbert, Lieutenant Colonel Keith Macksoud, Lieutenant Colonel Robin Wilkinson, Major Peter Russo, Staff Sergeant Paul Schunk, Captain Amanda Rudick, Sergeant Joshua Colon, Sergeant Richard Monaco, Lieutenant Colonel Tita Rafanan, Lieutenant Colonel Joann Kimmich, Lieutenant Colonel Peg Haggerty, Colonel Tom Cook, Sergeant First Class Mike Liddell, Colonel Brian Campbell, Staff Sergeant George Balzano, Lieutenant Colonel Judy Mendelsohn, Major Linda Magaraci, Colonel Mary-Ellen Murphy, Major Dennis Lauro, Major Steve Caravana, Lieutenant Colonel Bernie George, Lieutenant Colonel Majema Massenbury Corry, Sergeant Ray Murray, Colonel Ray Murray, Sergeant Brandon Hunsaker, Sergeant Jonas Bradshaw, Master Sergeant Dave McClory, Staff Sergeant Kim Mika, Major Kevin McMorrow, Sergeant Jameson O'Berry, Captain Brian Landry, and Sergeant Michelle Waterson. Finally, Sergeant First Class Mike Williams and the late Sergeant First Class Mike Williams (best friends who coincidently had the same name) were dear buddies till the end. Thanks also to all the other soldiers who I had the privilege to serve with.

If you thought I left you out, Major Roger Boutin, I did it on purpose: I wanted to give you special recognition. You were my first company commander in Hanscom AFB and should have been in Iraq. You reminded me the most of Major Dick Winters. I would follow you into battle any day!

I miss my dear friend Sergeant First Class Joe Forcier, who died too young, but I have never forgotten what he told me the first day I joined the unit: "We NCOs run the corps, and if you want to be a good officer, listen to us." I haven't forgotten, Joe!

Nor will I ever forget Corporal Brian St. Germain, Specialist Matthew Grimm, or Sergeant First Class Brent Dunkleberger, who made the ultimate sacrifice for their country. As we Irish say:

May the road rise up to meet you.
May the wind be always at your back.
May the sun shine warm upon your face;
the rains fall soft upon your fields and until we meet again,
may God hold you in the palm of his hand.

There is one more thing, guys, as you head out on your last mission: Watch out for those cowboys! You are my heroes!

To all the hotels who have adopted my family through the years of my nephews' multiple hospitalizations, I thank you from the bottom of my heart. I especially want to thank David Gore from the Best Western next to Boston Children's Hospital; Mr. David Gibbons, Bernardine, Jerry, Mercedes, and Meghan from the Taj Boston; Urszula, Bertrand, the Club Girls, and executive staff of the Intercontinental Hotel Cleveland; GM and the magical staff of the Yacht and Beach Club in Disney; Diane Difazio and her staff at the Hyatt in Newport: we love you all so much. Thanks also to all at the Ritz-Carlton Hotels, especially

Deborah Howard and Simon Cooper, who have treated my nephews like royalty. And thanks to the former general manager Henri Boubée and his wife, Liane, from the Ritz in Boston—you let us know there are wonderful people in the world and that dreams do come true.

There are so many others who do so much to support the troops, such as Merav Brooks at HBO, who kept the care packages coming to Iraq; Maggie Balasco and Susan Lonardo, owners of the Last Stop Salon, who are my dear friends who supplied us with color and nail products in Iraq; and Maria Francis from Merle Norman Cosmetics, another good friend who made sure all of us looked pretty even in a war zone. Jim Kennedy, who owns Confections in Fall River, made sure I got plenty of his homemade truffles and goodies to give to my soldiers. Thank you all for always being there for me, especially Ellen Inglese, our Family Readiness member who passed away last year, who was like a mother to all of us. And I don't want to forget Katie Brower from the Boston office of Platinum American Express, who plans all our fabulous trips for our family.

Thank you also to Deb Cunha from the *Federal Hill Gazette;* Deb Ruggiero, host of "Amazing Women;" Kelly Kennedy from the *Army Times;* Kristen Holmstedt, author of *Band of Sisters;* Janet Boivin from the *Nursing Spectrum* magazine.

I have several close friends who have been with me for life: Linda (Pezza) and Bob Andrews, Elaine and John D'Antuono, Jeanette and the late Lew Hight, Donna and Joe Manion, Father Raymond Rafferty, Jackie Ruggeri, Janie (Varnum) and Harry Tutko, Ann and Arthur Zarrella. Thank you all for your love and support, especially to you "two" who know who you are and have been at my side through thick and thin.

To my extended family, the late George Luz Sr. and his wife, Delvina, you made me feel like a daughter right from the start. To Steve and Sue Luz and their children, Becky and Michelle, as well as Albert and Lana Miller and their children, Amy, Alana, Seth, Danny, and C.J.: you are my other family now, too, and I couldn't have married into a better one.

My parents, Margaret and Pat Corry, will forever be in my heart along with Aunt Mary, Uncle Bill, and Aunt Ellen. I miss you all every day, especially you, Mom, who made me realize the cup was always half full. You always said your guardian angel would be at my side in the best and worst of times, and now I know I have two watching out for me.

To my sister, Ellen-Ann, and her husband, Steve Higginbotham, and children, Kate (and her husband, Richie), Meg, Geoffrey, and Matthew; to my brother, Bill Corry, who inspired me to write this story after he called our newspaper, and his wife, Karen; to my brother, Jack Corry, and his wife, Toni, and children, John Patrick (and his wife, Jennifer), Ryan, and little Mary; all I can say is: together still through it all! As a soldier I'd die for my country, but for my sister and brothers I want to live more every day to be with them and see their children and their children's children grow up. Along with my husband, they are the most important people in my life; I love them more than anything, and they have always been my heroes.

To that younger man from West Warwick, Rhode Island, who I told on my wedding day he would always be number three (after my parents) but who has now become my number one: My parents told me a husband should always come first, but I didn't initially believe them because I never dreamed I could love someone as much as I love you. You will be my endless love always and forever!

Finally, I'd like to say to my wonderful husband, George, and my family and friends: this is your story, too, because I am who I am from knowing and loving you.

ABOUT THE AUTHOR

COLONEL SUSAN LUZ is the highest-ranking soldier in the 399th Combat Support Hospital, an Army Reserve unit based out of Massachusetts. In 2007, she won the Bronze Star for meritorious service while in Iraq.

Trained as a nurse, she has lived a life devoted to public service and has worked in inner-city schools, jails, and adolescent psychiatric wards.

A former Peace Corps volunteer to Brazil, she holds a nursing degree from the University of Rhode Island and a master's degree in public health from Boston University.

Susan is no stranger to military circles. Her father was a World War II veteran who served under General George S. Patton. Her father-in-law is the late George Luz Sr., who was portrayed by actor Rick Gomez in the HBO miniseries *Band of Brothers*, based on Stephen Ambrose's best-selling book by the same name.

Susan lives with her husband, George Luz Jr., in Rhode Island.

ABOUT THE COLLABORATIVE AUTHOR

Marcus Brotherton is a journalist and collaborative writer. He is the author of *We Who Are Alive and Remain: Untold Stories from the Band of Brothers* and the coauthor of *Call of Duty*, with Lieutenant Buck Compton. He lives with his wife and children in Washington State.